"Lacewing"

"Red Fox"

T0244137

At
Home
with
Nature

At Home with Nature

A Guide to Sustainable, Natural Landscaping

JOHN GIDDING

Countryman Press

An Imprint of W. W. Norton & Company
Celebrating a Century of Independent Publishing

To my mom, Irene Kaino, for her love of art.
To my dad, John Gidding, for his love of history.

Contents

Introduction

Cedar, and Pine, and branching palm,
a Sylvan scene!
And as the ranks ascend shade above shade,
a woody theatre of stateliest view.
—*Paradise Lost (1667), John Milton*

I grew up astride the Bosporus and received a secondary education on an Alp. Perhaps my interest in nature was briefly awakened then, trading back and forth exotic sea passages for mountains. Nor would this interest have been inconsistent with my burgeoning love for architecture and my city, but Istanbul is treeless* and I first learned to love neighborhoods for their concrete and stone, their history and heritage, and their architectural diversity. By the time I showed up at Yale and Harvard, I knew I would study architecture.

Nature's inspiration first came in the form of my first job after graduate school, at a landscape architecture firm in New York City. Michael Van Valkenburgh had been at the forefront of ecological urbanism since 1982 and was busy presenting award-winning visions for the Brooklyn Bridge Park and Union Square when he gave me my first practical experience applying ecology to landscape design. I was on the team tasked with developing a design for the rooftop of the Washington, DC, headquarters of the American Society of Landscape Architects. The design called for two 10-foot-tall waves of vegetation, facing one another—a horizon rediscovered, cradling views of the city. The plant selection was purposefully broad as part of a long-term study of their felicity, one of the extended educational goals of the project, and were studied, photographed, and even kept on a webcam stream. The plants native to the mid-Atlantic region thrived compared with some of the foreign fronds, which required irrigation. An invaluable early lesson.

My second wakeup call came in a bamboo field in Zhejiang province. I was in China in 2007, choosing a diverse array of bamboo species for a pavilion at the upcoming Beijing Olympics. The pavilion was to be encircled with cascading bamboo gardens, some as tall as 60 feet high. China, also known as the Bamboo Kingdom, has over half of the world's native bamboo species, some 500 in all. Over three intensive excursions, I came in contact with many regional horticulturists as they led me through forests of bamboo, explaining how these forests have been sustained

* Only 1.5% of Istanbul is public green space (parks and gardens), the lowest of 44 cities in the *World Cities Culture Report*, 2013–14. New York has 14%, Paris 9.4%. Moscow leads with 54%.

and harvested for generations, their health maintained. Given that the Chinese have been cultivating bamboo for well over 3,000 years, their horticulturists are often called upon to distinguish between bamboo native to a region and those native to other regions, the former being essential for the health of the forest, the latter less so. Because the cultivation of some bamboo species was so ancient, a horticulturist's knowledge of a region's biological and human history seemed essential to a full understanding of the imperatives of the regional ecology. Another invaluable lesson. I visited a number of China's famous gardens and parks and have admired their landscaping techniques ever since.

Whatever may have been the fruits of my extensive education and brief apprenticeships in the world of architecture and urban design were quickly ripened when I decided to portray a fully fledged landscape architect on reality television. It was my circumstance to portray mastery of a profession I hadn't mastered, but the limited scope of work for TV design was such that I could do my research. My first few seasons of TV were spent redesigning front yards, restoring facades, and bringing some color into suburban neighborhoods. My focus was skewed toward the architecture. The landscapes were mostly new lawns, the kind that comes in rolls and makes all the mud disappear the last day of shooting. Not only was it great for TV production, but lawns were also what the homeowners, the networks, and the advertisers were requesting, and they came with accessories like irrigation systems, lawnmowers and glyphosate to kill weeds.

I'd like to say the muse of environmentalism had begun to sing so urgently that rather than changing out dead lawns for new rolls of sod week after week, I finally started to adopt landscaping techniques that respected the environment. It wasn't the case. My excuse is that I hadn't yet seen an alternative that could replace the suburban ideal. Instead, I would speak with local nurseries about which plants would thrive at our project site and insert a few native hedge-rows here and there.

During filming in Atlanta, I would sometimes find myself close enough to the Chattahoochee forest, where a river winds through the city's suburbs, to take a walk along the riverbank, sketchbook in hand. By a fluke of urban amnesia, this part of the Chattahoochee had been spared Atlanta's rapid development. With the forest intact, the river ran cool and clear. It was as John Milton described, "a Sylvan scene."* My sketches of the clusters of trees leading down to the river, the curving lines of riparian shrubs and grasses around them, and their natural clearings, became the vision of a native landscape that started to coalesce in my mind as one that could reunite suburban yards with the natural world by sheer dint of its sylvan charms.

The TV work brought me into the homes and gardens of neighborhoods across the nation, and I developed a deep fondness for suburbia. It was initially foreign, with a litany of rules and regulations set by HOAs and neighborhood committees, but with architectural vitality, enormous acreage, and spending power. I was also traveling throughout the states as a guest speaker at Home & Garden shows, treating each Q&A session like a laboratory of home-owning concerns in my quest to come up with new presentations. I came away convinced of the revelation I knew would not be welcome among those steeped in the tradition of lawn maintenance; to restore the degraded habitat upon which the suburbs had been erected, their inhabitants had to start hearing the growing chorus for native plants. Like Darwin, I have hesitated long before making my views public.**

"Black throated Blue Warbler"

Native plants, having evolved over untold millennia, have established a self-regulating ecosystem that protects them from disease, and they require no more water than is provided by the region's normal precipitation. *At Home with Nature* is a step-by-step guide by which suburban homeowners can design, with native plants, sustainable, beautiful landscapes for their own property. A key element of this sylvan style of landscaping will be the use of a greater number of trees than are usually found in a suburban yard, leading to a landscape that is aesthetically pleasing, in harmony with and supportive of the local environment.

The future health of our own habitats, and that of many species of wildlife, depends upon our capacity to adopt responsible strategies of landscape design, allowing a mix of spaces for people and wildlife, without taxing limited resources. Hearing the alarms of impending climate disasters nationwide, American suburbs are becoming newly receptive to bold design ideas, and at a time when they are in a unique position to meet the challenge. The time is now.

---

*   Sylvan, meaning: "of the forests or groves." Etymology: From the Latin "Sylvan" meaning forest glade; Sylvanus being the Roman god of forests, glades, and fields.
**   Having himself adventured and returned with a conviction, Darwin felt that believing in evolution was like confessing to a murder and hesitated for almost 20 years before making his views public.

PART I

Origins

CHAPTER 1

The Problem with Grass

"Plants recommend themselves to us by their taste, their fragrance, or their beauty, and so invite us to make repeated trials of their virtues: but, on the other hand, the properties of those which remain to be described, furnish us with abundant proof that nothing has been created by Nature without some purpose to fulfill, unrevealed to us though it may be."
—*The Natural History* (77AD), Pliny the Elder

AFTER WANDERING in the grass deserts of suburban properties chosen for reality TV makeovers, I had a vision. I came to see the grass lawn as a false god, worshipped by suburbanites, who religiously manicured a patch of green grass, of singular type, with no weeds, and who lavished libations of poisonous chemicals on their green altars. To test whether those who were purposely poisoning the earth held different views than my own, I have tried replacing turf grass with native shrubs and ground covers. Alas, the dearth of trees in suburban settings is without remedy in the context of a quick TV makeover. While the more ecologically minded homeowners were responsive to my efforts, those addicted to mowing saw my grassless vision as apostasy.

Instead of keeping to traditional landscape design, which focuses on the architecture as seen from the curb, I placed the accent on the landscape itself by planting small rows of interlocking shrubs between whatever trees happened to be in the yard. In so doing, I felt that the juxtaposition of the trees with the shrub-rows provided far more visual interest than the usual shrub-rows planted under the house's front windows.

It also separated the yard into zones too small for mowing, allowing for wildflower patches or woven patches of mixed ground cover. Often, my shrubbery tactics allowed me to place a bench in the front yard, close to where the trees met the shrub-rows, an element that became a signature item for my TV work. My feeble efforts to defy traditional landscaping notwithstanding, I was able to experiment with different arrangements of regional native plants. More important, I was given ample opportunity to discuss arrangements of native trees, shrubs, and ground covers with the experienced personnel of the plant nurseries (who were also doing much of the actual landscaping for the shows).

A decade of working for television shows and private clients has given me time to formulate a new approach to landscape design for the American suburb: an approach that fully excludes the use of turf grass, using only native plants, and emphasizes trees yet still conforms to the strictures and codes that govern the maintenance of suburban properties. Let us refer to this approach as ***sylvan landscaping***. As a prelude to a better understanding of the need for a sylvan landscape, it is necessary to understand just how the grass lawn secured such a foothold in suburbia. Going forward, my use of the term "grass" or "turf grass" specifically refers to those non-native species of grasses that are almost exclusively used for lawns.

Not one of the types of grass commonly used for suburban lawns, such as Kentucky blue grass, rye grass, or Bermuda grass, are native to the Americas, but rather to Europe, Asia, or Africa. When grown in America, these foreign grasses all require a toxic mix of fertilizers, herbicides, and pesticides, not to mention constant irrigation, to stay green. Even when green, these grasses do little for the local wildlife and often damage the roots of native trees. Over the course of the past 70 years, the total acreage of land devoted to suburban yards has increased at an unparalleled rate and the upkeep of this ocean of toxic grass has estranged suburban lands from the natural world from which they sprang.

GRASS ROOTS

After World War II, as America's population increased and the economy boomed, suburbs were carved out of the fields and forests surrounding the towns. A new aesthetic was needed with urgency. Grass lawns became entwined in the social fabric of America due to their European roots. In Europe, lawns were an early form of conspicuous consumption, signs their owners could afford to dedicate ground to aesthetic rather than agricultural purposes— and signs, too, that their owners, in the days before lawnmowers lessened the burden of grass shearing, could afford scythe-wielding peasants to do that labor. The wealthier of the early English settlers had brought these class notions with them to the New World.

The rise of the lawn as the preeminent feature of American suburbs can be traced back

to the preaching of America's patron saints of landscaping, Robert Downing and Frederick Olmsted. Robert Downing wrote: "Essential to a perfect garden was an expanse of grass mown into softness like velvet." Frederick Olmsted had created Riverside, a community with a shared fenceless lawn—a unified democratic lawn—that gave every homeowner a patch of grass to mow and maintain. Heated by centuries of English colonialism and fired by democratic ideals, how could these lawn enthusiasts appreciate the beauty of America's native plants and trees? Instead, they perceived expanses of mown grass as a status symbol with trees and shrubs as edge garnish. Their good word spread like weeds amongst the bourgeois and ultimately took root in the middle-class psyche.

When gold came to the United States in the 1880s, it became popular very quickly. By 1915, the US Department of Agriculture was collaborating with the United States Golf Association to find the right combination of grasses that would produce a lawn suitable across the broad American climate. Bermuda grass from Africa, bluegrass from Europe, and a mix of fescues and bent grasses from Asia were included in the research, but not, it seems, a single species of American grass. An enthusiastic proselytizer for the *good grass* ideology was the American Garden Club, who convinced homeowners that it was their civic duty to maintain beautiful and healthy lawns composed of good grass, famously defining a good grass lawn as one "mown to a height of an inch and a half, uniformly green, neatly edged and without weeds."* By the 1950s, suburbanites believed in the sanctity of grass and were embarking upon weekend mowing quests for the Holy Grail of the perfect lawn.

Riding the crest of this grass wave was Abraham Levitt, the creator of Levittown, arguably America's first suburban community. Levitt declared that "no single feature of a suburban residential community contributes as much to the charm and beauty of the individual home and the locality as well-kept lawns." By the 1960s, a well-maintained lawn—luxuriously lush, implying leisure, and conferring a higher status upon all who mowed—came to represent a social triumph of another kind: the perceived order of the disciplined suburban middle class over the proletariat's squalor in the city.

Levittown spawned a species of terrestrial development known today as tract housing, wherein multiple similar homes are built on a tract (area) of land that is subdivided into individual lots. These housing developments, with their colorfully named winding streets and cul-de-sacs, float upon a vast turf-grass sea. The size of this sodden sea will only increase as single-family zoning (one lot for one home) remains gospel in America, embraced by homeowners and local governments in their efforts to protect residential neighborhoods from denser development nearby. Single-family zoning will continue apace as most American cities still mandate that the majority of its available residential land be given over to building detached single-family homes. The average lot size for a new single-family home sold in the United States in 2013 was 0.35 acres, some 15,500 square feet, of which an average of 60% is blanketed with grass. Today, turf grass covers over 65,000 square miles of American soil, an area about the size of Florida and increasing every year.

THE PROBLEM WITH GRASS

The grass lawn has become so much a part of the suburban landscape that it is difficult to see it as something that was invented after the war.

*   Source: American-lawns.com

The enormous popularity of golf also played its part, one lawn-care fanatic describing as ideal "a beautifully striped lawn mowed tight like a golf course fairway."

The extent of the environmental damage grass has wrought upon the United States is staggering. Grass is our most irrigated crop, uselessly consuming over 30% of America's precious drinking water. Americans grow three times more inedible turf grass than edible corn. In addition, 70 million pounds of pesticide are spread annually over this gigantic lawn, killing birds and bees, polluting the water, and reducing the life spans of children, pets, and wildlife. Adding insult to this injury are the estimated 40 million lawnmowers that consume some 80 million gallons of gasoline per year, with each single mower polluting about the same as a new car. Then there is the impure waste to dispose of. Mowing the average lawn generates about 1,500 pounds of clippings per year, and given the amount of labor, herbicides, pesticides, fertilizers, and water it took to produce such waste, the disposal of these poisoned clippings then clogs landfills, adding insult to injury. How did America get itself in such an awful place?

The other problem with grass lawns is aesthetic. The grass lawn creates an estrangement from place: it is not a response to the landscape so much as an idea imposed upon it—all flat, all green, all the time—a condition that does not exist in nature. Nor does grass flourish under trees, and trees—which are essential for the health of the environment—rarely receive a sufficient place in housing developments. Still, an undeniable social benefit of the communal green carpet was that it became the common denominator; every resident's contribution to its regular upkeep carried real communal significance.

The ecological movements that irregularly oppose this burgeoning grass swathe lack the organization to counter the lawn-care lobby, and rarely address what replacement landscape would step in as suburbia's new aesthetic. Instead, many of these movements fob off the aesthetic responsibility on mother nature in the vain hope that she would quickly transform any jumbled selection of native plants into a sylvan landscape. While nature, over the course of decades of benign neglect, might well indeed accomplish these lofty ends, the needs of the suburban homeowner are generally more immediate. Nor do these movements consider means of overcoming the myriad of city and state property maintenance codes designed to keep the turf-grass lawn intact and regularly mown. Finally, there was a financial problem these enthusiasts failed to appreciate, the property's value was inextricably tied to its perceived appearance.

SYLVAN LANDSCAPING

The anti-lawn arguments of toxicity, habitat destruction, and resource depletion are all sound; if the perfect American lawn is seen for what it is, an expensive field of poison estranged from nature, what options are available to the ecologically inclined suburbanite? What landscaping techniques could they use to keep their land beautiful but beneficial to the environment? Clearly, traditional landscaping is out. No-mow alternatives of just letting the grass grow are not viable within the social context of suburbia or permitted under most existing property maintenance codes. While a pell-mell infusion of native plants onto the existing landscape will resolve many of the problems faced by bugs, birds, and small animals, this tactic lacks a cohesive aesthetic and will also run afoul of the maintenance codes. What, then, can mitigate the ecological disaster that turf grass has brought to the suburbs?

The answer to this question is to replace the turf grass with a thought-out and well-planned landscape composed of native trees, shrubs, and ground cover, a design that takes into account a dramatic increase in the number, kinds, and sizes of trees. By means of such landscaping, it remains possible for suburbia to reconcile itself with nature.

Fortunately, the movement toward the use of native plants to restore a toxic landscape is a growing one. But what is lacking in this movement is a method of design suitable for suburbanites who wish to live at home, with nature, in an aesthetically pleasing atmosphere and in the presence of native plants and wildlife. It is for this ecologically oriented suburban populace that I am proposing a method of designing a landscape that will meet the following social, aesthetic, and ecological objectives.

Social Objective

The American suburb owes much of its desirability to our appreciation of community and neighborliness. We take as an index of character the willingness and capacity of our neighbors to observe the specific rules of our developments. This is not by chance. The rigid conventions governing an individual's relationship to their property have been spelled out in some detail since the very first suburban development: Abraham Levitt's Levittown, where, by covenant, the original settlers agreed to mow their lawns once a week between April and November. Today, HOAs often impose steep fees and penalties on anyone unwilling to follow their neighborly advice, while immediate neighbors fret about their property values until the offending lawn-owner is brought to heel.

If you happen to live outside a planned community, with free reign over your land, consider yourself free to embrace the sylvan style without much thought as to how you might convince your neighbors of your benevolence. For everyone else, neighborly opinions must be taken into consideration and mollified during the installation of a sylvan landscape. You will find more than a few friends, some right next door, holding a dim view of your efforts. Ecological arguments must be put forth, if not to immediately convince, then at least to temporarily mollify neighbors while your new landscape takes root. Sylvan landscaping is not as simple to install as turf grass, as any newly planted ground cover will look weedy or messy, especially to the keen turf-grass eye. But given a chance to establish itself—and thoughtfully planned out—will evolve into a naturally beautiful carpet your neighbors will appreciate. Regrettably, though luckily for our current effort, the second decade of the 21st century has few who would directly challenge anyone's investment in the environment. While the Levittown suburbanite in you may have an irrepressible urge to blend in with the neighbors, remember there are benefits to standing out, too. Not the least of which will be your burgeoning property values when established native landscapes outshine the brown lawns of tomorrow.

Aesthetic Objective

To visualize the sylvan aesthetic, first consider the Middle English word "laune," which meant, as does sylvan, a glade or an open space in a forest or woods. Then imagine a laune to be a space bordered by larger trees interspersed with smaller trees, shrubs, wildflowers, fescues, and possibly a house. The house should not be the unique focal point in a sylvan landscape but rather a counterpoint. Such an aesthetic could be achieved on a suburban property by placing the larger trees to the sides and back of the property, the smaller understory trees toward the center, and with all the trees visually linked to each other by shrub-rows. The resulting pattern of trees and shrub-rows has an open maze quality that provides more interesting views of the landscape, whether looking out or looking in. These kinds of tree and shrub arrangements will produce a landscape that is complete unto itself, regardless of the characteristics or position of the house. More important, the aesthetic of a so-designed sylvan landscape can embrace the community standards. It does not wall off the property, but rather gives everyone natural vistas to contemplate from their own property. Finally, the open maze pattern of trees and shrubs offers the homeowner a degree of privacy, and a capacity to be creative with the captured spaces within.

While the communal lawn has long served as a common denominator, what happens when the ground beneath the grass begins to shift and conscientious suburbanites start to embrace the environment? Can a new aesthetic be embraced before a decline in water resources? Can we shrug off the influences of aristocrats and golf clubs in time? While no landscape can ever be perfect in the eyes of all, a sylvan landscape, by keeping the lines of sight between properties open and attractive while reinvigorating the local ecology respects both the social balance and the environment.

Ecological Objective

The ecological problem starts when developers, in order to construct profitable suburban housing projects, begin by stripping the topsoil and removing the existing plants before embarking on the construction phase. Because turf grass fares badly in shade and a sod lawn can be completely installed in a single day, developers do not plant trees unless they are required or have meagerly budgeted to do so. The first owners may add a tree here or a shrub there, but their focus will be on keeping the newly minted turf grass in prime condition rather than replenishing the recently destroyed ecosystem.

Water, once seen as an inexhaustible commodity, has become a scarce and precious resource. As natural resources diminish, the traditional focus of landscaping, which has been to enhance the house and please the owner, is finally shifting toward what is best for the planet and agreeable to the owner. It will soon become evident to the adherents of turf grass that they are slipping down an inclined slope at the bottom of which lies only one thing: no more irrigation. Without regular irrigation, turf grass will brown, wither, and die. What is surprising is the length of time it is taking for the municipal fathers to come to grips with this reality and enact policies obliging suburbanites to adopt a form of landscaping that does away with both turf grass and irrigation. True, turf-grass lawns are useful for those interested in playing badminton, croquet, or hosting large social events, but there are other possible venues for these activities. Native trees, disdained and neglected over the past century, need to be reintroduced and underplanted with native shrub layers that are absent from most managed landscapes. Hopefully, one can expect, in the not-too-distant future, a scenario wherein lawnmowers are replaced by pruning shears, and where the neighbors do not war upon those who do not mow. When this ecological revolution does come around, and it has already begun in some states, real commercial value will accrue to a property that has a mature, aesthetically pleasing, eco-friendly landscape.

A BRIEF HISTORY OF MAN'S INFLUENCE ON THE NORTH AMERICAN ENVIRONMENT

Around 25,000 years ago, North America was in the grip of its last ice age. Northern regions were covered in ice and the more southerly regions were wetter and colder than they are today. The native ranges of plants tended to follow the physical north—south avenues dictated by the Rocky and Appalachian mountain ranges. Climate had a similar effect, as the plants evolving in the north were stopped by the heat, and those evolving in the south were stopped by the cold. When the climate warmed, plants were able to respond to environmental change by a phenomenon known as range migration. Individual plants, of course, cannot pick up and leave when conditions get tough, but the wildlife does. And as goes the wildlife, from the megafauna to the bees, so goes the seed dispersal toward the more favorable climate, a process that continues today. As plants and wildlife migrate into new territory, the biodiversity adapts and the ecosystems mutate until equilibrium is achieved.

At some point, man made his presence felt. The Anthropocene is said to be the epoch when human activity became the dominant influence on the earth's environment. As the impact of human activity on the different continents has been irregular, there is no secular agreement for the start date of the Anthropocene, and dates ranging from 11,650 BC to 1944 AD have been suggested. What is sure is that, as humans came to the New World, the environment was seriously modified by social and political factors that confounded the ecological balance.

There have been three distinct migrations of people into North America. Homo sapiens had first come to the continent some 20,000 years ago, when peoples from Siberia managed to pass overland to what is now Alaska. The next arrival dates to 1492 when Columbus made landfall in the Caribbean and the European colonization of the New World began. The last great coming began in 1776, after the 13 original colonies declared their independence from England and wave upon wave of immigrants came to the United States to fuel its westward expansion.

The Siberian bands of hunters and fishers who first crossed over the Bering Strait via a land bridge had likely seen it surface at various times during the last Ice Age. Heading east from a cold desolate place, these nomads pushed ever onward toward more accommodating environments. As they migrated farther south, glaciers melted* and the sea levels rose again. With the Western Hemisphere again separated from Asia, human influx was paused. All American Indians are descended from these original Siberian nomads. Not long after the land bridge disappeared, many species of America's larger fauna like mastodons and woolly mammoths—whether due to climate change, overhunting by the nomads, or combinations of both—had become extinct.

As the megafauna became scarce and cold-weather flora retreated north, tribes began to prey upon smaller animals, to catch fish, and to consume a wider array of plant foods, building seasonal residences along waterways and developing systems of trade. Isolated for millennia, the roving Archaic peoples coalesced into larger tribes as they migrated all the way to the southern tip of South America, forming complex civilizations and reli-

---

* At the end of the last Ice Age, some 14,000 years ago.

gions along the way. Throughout the Americas maize (corn), squash, and beans formed the basis of agriculture. The absence of livestock in the Western Hemisphere, notably horses, had limited agriculture by preventing the large-scale plowing of fields but nonetheless, by the time the Europeans arrived the Western Hemisphere contained imposing cities connected by roads, irrigation systems, and trade networks.

Confrontation with the Europeans brought a close to the growth of indigenous societies and, in many cases, an end to the societies themselves. To European eyes, the continent to be explored was immense and filled with hostile savages, but given the great distance between Europe and America, coupled with the precarity of 16th-century ocean voyaging, the indigenous peoples were not subdued overnight. One hundred years after its discovery, the shape of the American continent remained largely a mystery; California, for example, was thought to be an island. Yet, given all obstacles, the European exploration and settlement of the Americas proceeded with remarkable speed.

The European invaders were as gentle to the environment as they were kind to the indigenous people. The vast, unexplored lands before them, thanks to a combination of disease, advanced technology, and avarice, succumbed to their exploitation. And more settlers kept coming. By the middle of the 18th century, Dutch, British, and German settlers had permanently established themselves along the Atlantic coast, building towns, clearing forests, and introducing new crops and livestock. Slowly at first, but with ever-increasing speed, the environment between the Atlantic Ocean and the Allegheny Mountains began to change. By 1776, when the coastal states declared their independence from England based on the idea that "all men are created equal," the Atlantic Frontier had grown to include the Appalachian Mountains.

As the new republic expanded ever westward, army posts were interspersed along the line of each successive frontier. Ostensibly for the protection of the settlers from the hostilities of the indigenous tribes, each new army post served as a wedge to open up tribal country and provide a nucleus for a new settlement, and the expansion of the western frontier fueled the construction of more and more military installations. The acquisition of land from Mexico in 1848 spurred the need for a constant military presence from the Rio Grande River to the Pacific. Each new expansion displaced the indigenous tribes, and any who fought back lost.

The waves of settlement, like ocean waves shaping stone and sand, rolled one after the other upon the environment and continue to this day. The first pioneers were, much like the land's original inhabitants, hunters and subsistence farmers, with small ecological footprints. Next came emigrants who purchased lands, cleared forests, grew fields, built roads, dammed rivers, and threw bridges over streams. Finally, the men of capital and enterprise came as towns turned into cities surrounded by the extensive agricultural fields that ultimately gave way to today's suburban housing developments. The resulting degradation of the ecology of the United States has been proportional to its populations, size, and density[*]. The good news is, you're about to plant some trees. Others will follow.

---

[*]   The American population was 250,000 in 1700, 5 million in 1800, 76 million in 1900, and 282 million by the year 2000. It is 331 million today.

CHAPTER 2

The Humanization of the Environment

"The second region (of the United States) is more varied on its surface, and better suited to the habitation of man. Two long chains of mountains divide it from one extreme to the other, the Alleghany *[sic]* ridge takes the form of the Atlantic Ocean; the other is parallel with the Pacific. The space between these two chains of mountains contains 1,341,649 square miles. Its surface is therefore about six times as that of France. This vast territory, however, forms a single valley, one side of which descends gradually from the rounded summits of the Alleghany Mountains,* while the other rises in an uninterrupted course toward the top of the Rocky Mountains. At the bottom of the valley flows an immense river, into which the various streams issuing from the mountains fall from all parts."
—*Democracy in America* (1835), Alexis de Tocqueville

ALEXIS DE TOCQUEVILLE accurately delineated the three regions of the United States where mountain ranges, extending from the north to the south of the continent, first posed a barrier to plant migration and then to human migration. These three vast vertical regions lie between the Atlantic and the Appalachians, the Appalachians and the Rockies, and the Rockies and the Pacific. These three regions are, in turn, cut horizontally by cold, temperate, and hot climatic divisions, as well as the rainy and the arid. All of these factors had an impact on the regional density of human settlement and accompanying degradation of the environment. The Plant Hardiness Zone Map, compiled by the United States Department of Agriculture (USDA), offers a broad synthesis of these factors. The hardiness of plants—not entirely unlike that of human beings—is based on their ability to survive subfreezing temperatures or lack of rainfall. Given that population growth and industrialization generally follow agricultural development and that agriculture is more successful in the temperate and rainy regions, these are the regions whose environments suffered the most.

The full history of the effects of human settlement on the environment of what would become the United States can never be written, as we know too much about it. Our forefathers have accumulated so vast a quantity of information on centuries past that the digital com-

* In the early 19th century, there was no general agreement on the use of Alleghenies versus Appalachians, but both referred to the same long chain of eastern mountains.

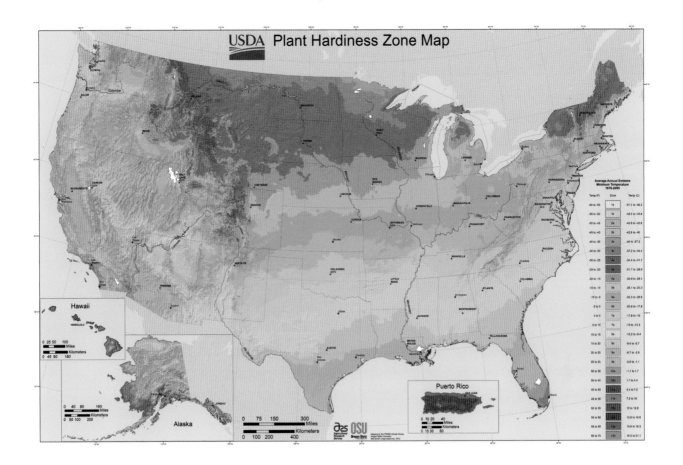

mons of the Library of Congress has quailed before it. So it is not by a scrupulous narration that this researcher can hope to depict such a singular epoch but rather by a subtler strategy. I have chosen to focus on six regions suggested by geography and climate: (1) Northeast, (2) Southeast, (3) Midwest, (4) Gulf Coast, (5) West, and (6) Northwest; and to analyze each region through the prism of a subregion and an adjacent city. My choice of the subregion and city, within each region, has not been determined by a desire to construct a theory of landscaping, but by the simple motives of convenience and art. And so, in the history of a city on a river, in the hills, on the prairie, in a swamp, in a valley, and on the edge of a bay, I have sought to examine those environmental changes that took my fancy. I hope that the following helps illuminate the unique environmental features of each region while also providing some historical context of how these regions evolved into what they are today.

NORTHEAST: CONNECTICUT RIVER WATERSHED
(HARTFORD, CONNECTICUT)

"Seeing this, I can realize how this country appeared when it was discovered. Such were the oak woods in which the Indian treaded hereabouts. Such a wood must have had a peculiar fauna to some extent. . . . We have but a faint conception of a full-grown oak forest stretching uninterrupted for miles, consisting of sturdy trees from one to three and even four feet in diameter, whose interlacing branches form a complete and uninterrupted canopy. Many trunks old and hollow, in which wild beasts den, hawks nesting in the dense tops, and deer glancing between the trunks, and occasionally the Indian with a face the color of the faded oak leaf."
—*Observations* (journal entry of November 10, 1860), Henry David Thoreau

Such were Henry David Thoreau's inaccurate observations while walking through what he believed to be one of New England's last parcels of virgin forest. Thoreau had failed to understand the impact American Indians had on New England's coastal landscape, for these indigenous peoples had been altering the forests for thousands of years before the Europeans had stumbled onto the New World.

The idea that the New World was a pristine wilderness before the Europeans arrived was a myth, and the visitor from Walden Pond was steeped in this myth. The canopy closure and forest tree density that Henry David Thoreau mistook for virgin forest developed only after the ruin of the native population.

Studies have shown that the white oak was a foundational species of tree in New England's precolonial forests; that the hemlock and American chestnut became the dominant species when and where they could; and that the maple, black elm, and white pine were always abundant. The composition of the old forests changed when the colonists, moving slowly inland from the coast, cleared forests for agriculture and built small subsistence farms along the fertile bottomland near the rivers.

Evolution of the Connecticut River Watershed

The Connecticut River, New England's counterpart to the Mississippi, is the longest river in the eastern United States. Arising just below the Canadian border, the Connecticut River flows southward though the states of New Hampshire, Vermont, and Massachusetts, before bisecting Connecticut and discharging into Long Island Sound 45 miles below Hartford.

By the early 1800s, the establishment of farms, beginning along the coast and up through the watershed of the Connecticut River, spread rapidly throughout New England as farmers began to supply food and wool to a rapidly growing nation. By 1820, less than 30% of New England remained forested.

New England's natural wildlife began to suffer as their forest-dependent species like bears, elk, and mountain lions lost their habitat, while other species like beavers and wild turkey were harvested for food and pelt. By 1860, much of the farmland had been exhausted, and its small, stony farms were unable to compete with the larger, more mechanized farms of the Midwest. After the Civil War, farming and deforestation came to an end with the opening of the western territories and the incentive of free land. The farms were abandoned, the farmers moved west, and before long the forests began to return.

The degradation of the New England environment resumed during the Industrial Revolution, which was at this time developing within the Connecticut River Valley a network of dams to supply power to the region's fledgling industries. The accompanying raw waste, dumped uncontrolled, destroyed the river's biological integrity, introducing large-scale industrial pollution to the entire watershed. The abuse of this watershed has continued right up to the end of the 20th century, prompting actress Katharine Hepburn, a proud resident of Hartford, to famously call the Connecticut River "the world's most beautifully landscaped cesspool."*

*   *The Long Tidal River* (1965) is a Connecticut River documentary film narrated by Katharine Hepburn.

2

SOUTHEAST: SOUTHERN APPALACHIANS
(ATLANTA, GEORGIA)

In 1831, the Supreme Court declined to rule upon the Cherokee Nation's petition to keep possession of their Georgia homeland. The Supreme Court's decision, or rather indecision, set in motion the machinery that would cause the Cherokees to be expelled from Georgia and set upon the Trail of Tears. The Court's ruling, delivering the forests of Northern Georgia to less scrupulous wards, is worth a read.[*]

Evolution of the Allegheny's Southern Forests

In pre-Columbian times, related indigenous tribes, styled the "Mississippians," lived in the river valleys east of the Mississippi and constructed large, earthen pyramids for religious, cultural, and social purposes. During the millennia prior to the European discovery of the New World, the Mississippians' relatively advanced culture slowly spread east, following the river valleys wherein they cleared large swaths of low-lying land for agricultural and settlement purposes. As the Mississippians' culture was primarily based upon river valley agriculture, they left forests in the Allegheny Mountains intact and covered with old-growth forests. This diverse forest had large trees, such as the oak and chestnut, that dominated the uppermost layers of vegetation.

The Cherokees also migrated into Georgia's river valleys where they, too, left the mountain forests in what was basically a primeval condition, subject to little or no human interference.

Even the English colonizers left the mountain forests largely as they were.

And so it was that the southern half of the Allegheny mountain forests remained relatively untouched until 1829, when gold was discovered in the mountains. The gold rush triggered the arrival of prospectors, hastened the disenfranchisement of the Cherokees, and exposed the forests to the hand of man. By the early 1840s gold had become difficult to find and, with the Cherokees being pushed off their land, many prospectors took to farming. These early farmers used the forest's timber and plant commodities for their own home consumption and used the open land for low-key subsistence agriculture. The homesteader's farms were generally half-forested, and the timber they logged was primarily used for their own homes, barns, and fences. When these settlers did engage in small-scale commercial logging, they used draft animals, and their techniques were sustainable, leaving the forest in a condition to be able to reproduce itself. These settlers

---

[*]   *Cherokee Nation v. Georgia*, 30 US Supreme Court, Pet. (1831)

also practiced what has become known as single tree selection, whereby trees to be cut are selected on the basis of diameter and condition; smaller and younger trees are retained to grow on to the next harvest, and the old-growth trees are left for future species' habitat. These early farmers had a respect for the land, and the land, in return, provided for them.

The Civil War forever changed the South. Alongside carpetbaggers came timber companies from the north buying up tens of thousands of acres of forest at rock-bottom prices. Beginning in the 1880s, thousands of acres of the Allegheny forest could be had from poor mountain farmers for a few dollars an acre. The new breed of timber extractors practiced large-scale industrial logging, using heavy machinery and clear-cutting in large tracts. Across once-pristine mountain streams they built splash dams, log structures that raised the water level high enough to back up a large quantity of cut timber. These temporary dams were then exploded in order to wash the timber far downstream in one enormous and instant flood. These logging techniques, still in use today, stripped almost every mountain watershed of its natural resources and wreaked havoc on the environment. As the forests were depleted, the number of lumber mills dropped drastically between 1909 and 1919, but iron ore mining was also contributing to the destruction of the forests. Speculators, chiefly northern industrialists, mined coal and iron and logged the ridges for timber to make charcoal for smelting the iron ore.

In 1924, Georgia's state geologist declared that the stripped forest landscape had lost its economic potential, making it a candidate for inclusion in the emerging national forest system in the Southeast. The present national forest system was established under the Weeks Act of 1911, which authorized a relatively new agency, the US Forest Service, to acquire land for forest reserves. To create a bulwark against irresponsible forestry practices, the Forest Service began purchasing surviving patches of old-growth forests, as well as overcut or over-farmed land, in the hope that some of these lands could be reforested for future timber needs.

Originally created to be a model of stewardship, the Forest Service employed many of the timbering practices it had originally opposed and logged almost all of the remaining old-growth forest by the end of World War II. Private land around the national forest also experienced a high degree of forest removal in the last few decades of the 20th century. Georgia alone lost almost 100,000 acres of forestland to urban development between 1990 and 2000, and the trend is expected to continue as Atlanta continues to sprawl ever northward. Fortunately, the Chattahoochee National Forest, once considered a primary source of forest products, is now a protected and highly valued forest because of the tourism dollars it brings to local communities, its recreational opportunities, and the clean water it provides to millions of downstream residents.

Georgia's Wildlife

In the spring of 1542, Hernando De Soto lay dying of fever in a forgotten Arkansas swamp, having explored the New World from Florida to the Mississippi River. Rather than go into the New World's dark night peacefully, and to the astonishment of his fellow conquistadores, De Soto proclaimed himself a god. At the time of De Soto's ascension, his earthly possessions consisted of 4 Indian slaves, 3 horses, and 700 hogs. While the fate of his slaves and horses has not yet transpired, his swine were early contributors to the Columbian Exchange. The hogs that managed to escape or otherwise avoid

probate became the ancestors of the feral pigs now found throughout the southeast. In less than 300 porcine generations, these invasive swine devolved into 5-foot-long savage boars, often weighing over 250 pounds, and whose upper tusks continually hone their razor-sharp lower tusks. Now called razorbacks because of their hair-covered backbones and bad tempers, they have insatiable appetites for plants and small mammals. Razorbacks are living monuments to the South's only self-proclaimed deity, fitting mascots for the University of Arkansas' football team, and unmitigated environmental disasters.

MIDWEST: MISSOURI TERRITORY
(ST. LOUIS, MISSOURI)

What was the New World like when Columbus arrived? The Admiral himself spoke of a terrestrial paradise: beautiful, green, fertile, teeming with birds, and peopled with carefree natives, a number of whom he enslaved. It is now an acknowledged fact that many of the landscapes the Europeans encountered during the 16th century had long been humanized and that the imprint of the indigenous peoples was both persistent and dramatic. What the Europeans did not realize was that the pinnacle of the native civilizations of North America had been realized, not on the coasts, but in the Mississippi Valley, and that the Mississippians had modified the landscape of America's great inland valley centuries before Columbus's landfall.

The Mississippian peoples were an agricultural society who lived in river valleys where periodic flooding replenished the soil's nutrients and kept their fields fertile. Their agricultural practices produced a surplus that had allowed them the time and leisure to master the arts and crafts that define and memorialize higher civilizations. Their larger cities were densely populated, complex, and symmetrically laid out around the bases of their large, earthen pyramids, much like Aztec cities in Mexico. Mercifully, the Mississippian civilization had waned and their pyramids had eroded into mounds before they could be decimated by contact with the Europeans.

Evolution of the Missouri Territory

The Mississippian's major city—named Cahokia at a later date—was situated just across the Mississippi River from what is now the city of St. Louis, Missouri. At its apex, around 1100AD, Cahokia covered 6 square miles or ground and had an estimated population of 40,000.[*] Enclosed within Cahokia's city limits were 120 man-made earthen mounds in a wide range of sizes, shapes, and functions. Cahokia faced the same material problems as do all large cities: a constant supply of food and water as well as how to manage their waste. There is much debate on how the Mississippians managed their resources. Did they live in harmony with nature with sustainable systems of resource management, or did they alter their environment to accommodate rises in population? While it is possible that a few outlying tribes lived in such harmony, it is certain that Mississippians living in the more populous centers did not. It is equally certain that they had dramat-

---

* Cahokia had the same population as contemporaneous London.

ically altered the landscape of the Mississippi Valley long before the Europeans arrived.

William Cronon, a prominent environmental historian, framed the resource management question this way: "the choice is not between two landscapes, one with and one without a human influence; it is between two ways of living, two ways of belonging to an ecosystem."* While the American Indians' use of fire was different from that of the European settlers, both relied upon fires to change the shape of the land for farming, grazing, or other development. The Mississippians burned parts of their ecosystems in order to produce a diversity of habitats, particularly to increase the boundaries of the prairies and the forests in order to allow for a greater diversity of plants and wildlife. The improvement of the habitat at these boundaries, referred to as the edge effect, allowed the Mississippians to produce the staples their society depended upon, thus providing greater security and stability. The first European settlers in the Mississippi Valley were more equipped for trade than the Mississippians were and were able to rely upon commerce with their homeland or other colonies for many of their staples. As a result of their mercantile possibilities, these settlers burned parts of their ecosystems to create greater uniformity for commercial agricultural activities, the bulk of which was destined for trade rather than local consumption.

---

*   *Changes in the Land: Indians, Colonists, and the Ecology of New England* (1983), William Cronon.

The purposeful fire history of the Ozark highlands and the Missouri plains demonstrates how human migration affects fire regimes. Subsequent to the demise of the Mississippians who regularly burned their fields, circa 1500AD, other migrating tribes slowly filled in the void and eventually took up agriculture on the abandoned sites. During the late 1700s, Cherokees began to migrate into the Ozarks after the European settlers started to displace them from their homelands in the southern Appalachians. By 1803 there were about 6,000 Cherokee living in southeast Missouri and northeast Arkansas. By 1820, the number of annually burned sites increased by 20%. In 1838, many more Cherokees settled in the Ozark region, after having been forcibly removed from their homelands by the US government, and the number of annually burned sites doubled. When the Civil War ended, migrations of settlers into Missouri caused initial decreases in the fire regime as they displaced the Cherokees and subsequent increases in fire regimes when the settlers began farming, further altering the pre-existing vegetative communities.

Forests

The settlers who followed on the heels of the Cherokees and occupied the Ozark Mountains were eventually styled "Ozarkers." The Ozarkers inexplicably decided not to follow their fellow Americans into the industrialized world but rather chose to keep to the older agrarian and cultural ways that they had inherited from their ancestors, poor Scottish and Irish immigrants for the most part. Beginning in the 1820s, migrants from Tennessee, Kentucky, and the western fringes of the Carolinas and Virginias pushed well beyond the pale of civilization and purchased or squatted upon small tracts of land along the river valleys of the Ozarks. They limited their agricultural practices to garden crops, relied on the surrounding woods for additional food and materials to build and heat their homes, maintained a relationship of non-intensive exploitation with the land and a system of barter and trade with their neighbors. Low-population density kept the exploitation of the forests minimal, allowing the local populace to utilize the hills and woods sustainably. Fires were set habitually by the Ozarkers to replenish and extend the grazing lands. While these fires extended the grasslands at the expense of the forests, a good annual burn removed unwanted vermin, snakes, and ticks, and also refreshed the growth of nutritive grasses for free-ranging livestock. Through the use of fire, the old forests were transformed into fields for open-range grazing and subsistence farming.

In the 1880s, large timber companies were moving to Missouri to harvest shortleaf pine and oak. The shortleaf pine was largely depleted by 1910, but the oak harvest continued. Ozarkers, with their older traditions of subsistence hunting, gathering, and basic farming, frequently resisted the efforts of both the timber companies and governmental agencies to bring modernization and industrial productivity to the region. Conservation ordinarily begins as a result of local self-determination, but, due in large part to the Ozarkers' legendary stubbornness, it developed later in Missouri than in the neighboring states. It was not until 1933 that the federal government created Missouri's first national forest.

Prairies

The great prairie that once dominated the central part of the United States can be categorized into three types: the tall grass prairie, situated near the Mississippi and Missouri river valleys; the mixed grass prairie, farther west; and the short grass prairie, situated to the east of the Rocky Mountains. The difference between each prairie type is a simple one to understand: the more annual precipitation the area receives, the taller the grass grows.

Studies have shown that one-third of Missouri's land mass, about 15 million acres, was once covered by tall grass prairie. This tall grass prairie was an ecosystem composed of a mosaic of warm-season grasses, flowering forbs, and shrubby prairie species that often grew over 6 feet tall, with few trees. This unique and complex ecosystem, sustained by fire and intense grazing by multitudes of buffalo, elk, antelope, and prairie dogs, limited the establishment of trees and the subsequent forest succession. Many of these prairie plants, particularly the grasses, are adapted to extreme conditions and are resistant to heat, cold, flooding, grazing, and fire. These prairie plants developed an unusually deep root system that built rich, deep soil over time. A large number of the prairie grasses are close relatives of corn, also a native plant. Key to the rise of the Mississippian civilization was their discovery that the unique properties of the prairies would support healthy and abundant food crops. In 1800, the tall grass prairie was virtually undisturbed, or at least it may have resembled what it used to be after the Mississippians had altered it.

Today, Missouri counts 276 myriad species of native grass and crop plants, often lovingly named. Out in the prairies, big bluestem grass, the most famous of the native grasses, has seed heads that resemble its nickname, "turkeyfoot." In drier upland areas, the short curly leaves are the giveaway for "poverty grass," and "nodding wild rye" is the common name for Canada wild rye, with its downward-curving seed heads. Missouri also has many species of sedge and rush, which people often think of as belonging to the same graminoid (grasslike) group. A local rhyme will help a budding eco enthusiast differentiate among them: "Sedges have edges, rushes are round, grasses are hollow with nodes—which have you found?"

However, thanks to John Deere's invention of the steel plow blade, prairies had been plowed into next-to-nothingness within 100 years. Like the buffalo before it, the tall grass prairie has nearly disappeared and what little is left has been torn into small pieces with settlements all across what was once just prairie. By the end of the 20th century, 99% of the original tall grass prairie had been plowed under and the remaining 80,000 acres were scattered about in tiny pieces, isolated tall grass islands in a sea of commercial agriculture and urban development. These tiny prairie islands lack the critical species of the wildlife community and are more like grass museums than thriving ecosystems.

We have a tendency to celebrate what is irretrievably lost rather than focus on what could possibly be saved, and so it is that Missourians celebrate Prairie Day in September. Restore the Prairie projects also exist, usually involving properties considerably larger than suburban yards and reintroducing controlled burnings.

Missouri's Wildlife

The Mississippi flyway, a bird migration route that generally follows the Mississippi and Missouri rivers, converges over the city of St. Louis. Migrating birds follow this route because there are no mountains or ridges of hills that block their path and good sources of food and water exist, or used to exist, over its entire length. Nearly 40% of all migrating North American waterfowl and shorebirds follow this route.

Missouri is also home to 13 species of carnivores, ranging from the least weasel, weighing a mere 2 ounces, to the black bear, weighing in at 240 pounds. Carnivore in the scientific sense of the word refers not simply to a species that eats meat, but to a species that belongs to the order *Carnivora* and whose members share a common ancestor and a heritage of meat consumption. The carnivore's identifying characteristics include enlarged canine teeth, three pairs of incisors on both top and bottom jaws, and molars with a modified shape for meat chewing. Carnivores are also territorial, marking the bounds of their territories with scent. Given that they exist at the top of the food pyramid, carnivores, vis-à-vis other species, are relatively rare. It requires vast ecosystems to sustain populations of large and medium-sized carnivores because of the considerable amounts of prey they need to consume to survive.

Yet not every carnivore feeds exclusively on protein. For instance, American black bears feed, for the most part, on nuts, berries, and other vegetation. To those who love Winnie-the-Pooh[*] or have purchased honey in plastic bear containers, it seems axiomatic that all bears love honey. America's black bears seem to be particularly adapted and adept at eating honey, because their thick fur repels the bees' stings, and they protect their tender noses by burying them in the honeycombs. But remember, only the invasive honeybee produces honey. Given that honeybees did not arrive in America until 1622, why do American black bears seem so adapted to eating honey? The answer is that black bears have always eaten entire beehives for their protein-rich larvae, but should they stumble upon a honeybee hive, the honey is the cherry on top.

[*]   *Winnie-the-Pooh* (1926), A. A. Milne.

GULF COAST: BIG THICKET
(HOUSTON, TEXAS)

Texas, the westernmost American state bordering the Gulf of Mexico, has four distinct physical regions. Incorporation of these four regions into a single state is often cited as the difference between human and physical geography. East Texas, the most humid of these four regions, is bordered on the west by the Trinity River (on a rough vertical line with Houston), on the north by the Red River (the Oklahoma border), on the east by the Sabine River (the Louisiana border), and on the south by the Gulf of Mexico. Most of East Texas's geography consists of piney woods and swampy marshes.

The Big Thicket, one of East Texas's most remarkable features, is a nearly impenetrable swamp that lies roughly 10 or 15 miles north of the Gulf Coast and between the city of Houston and the Sabine River. The Big Thicket is a unique ecosystem often referred to as America's Ark and considered to lie at the biological crossroads of North America.[*]

Evolution of the Big Thicket

In 1528, Cabeza de Vaca became the first European to see and explore the coast and interior of East Texas. He came to the Big Thicket after having been shipwrecked on Galveston Island, enslaved by the local populace, and then set free, along with three other survivors, to suffer and wander where they would. It took Cabeza de Vaca 8 years of much suffering and endless wandering[**] before he was able to get back to his own people near Mexico City. Once returned to Spain, his descriptions of the Big Thicket's loathsome insects, with indigenous people indiscriminately setting fire to the land, did little to attract the next generations of conquistadores, whose interests were more pecuniary than botanical. Nor did any of the local American Indian tribes make the Big Thicket their permanent home, although some hunting camps and sites of temporary use have been documented. The Spanish and French expeditions of the 17th century chose not to deal with the Big Thicket's enormous, impenetrable, and swampy forest, and their few settlements were all located at its semi-hospitable edges.

In the 1820s, the Mexican government, finally free of Spanish rule, promised free land to foreign settlers with the hidden intention of displacing the warring Apache and Comanche tribes, not without success. The first waves of US armed homesteaders who came to East Texas also avoided the Big Thicket and remained on its outskirts. In 1835, these armed

---

[*] *Nature Lovers' Guide to the Big Thicket* (1994), Howard Peacock.
[**] Estimated at 2,000 miles.

and newly minted Texans, led by Sam Houston, revolted against Mexico, seeking their own independence as the Republic of Texas (1836–46), then petitioned to become a part of the United States. When the Civil War broke out 15 years later, Texans seceded from the Union.

Many Texans, living near the Big Thicket, refused to fight for the Confederacy and hid within its quasi-impenetrable interior. The Confederate army set the cane break on fire in the vain hope of flushing them out. The Kaiser Burn Out,* as the fire was later styled, destroyed some 3,000 acres of pristine swamp.

When the Civil War ended, and the mid-19th-century lumber boom began, the destruction of the Big Thicket began in earnest. On the eve of its destruction, the Big Thicket covered an estimated 3.5 million acres, much of it in old-growth bald cypress and longleaf pine. After the harrow of industrial logging had passed over the Big Thicket, oil was discovered. By 1920, the old forest seemed doomed. What came to be a 50-year struggle to protect a portion of the Big Thicket for posterity began in 1927 with the formation of the East Texas Big Thicket Association. While the Association's lofty goals were never realized, some 85,000 acres, 2.5% of the original swamp, spread over six or seven parcels, was eventually saved.

What little remains of the Big Thicket today is considered one of the most biodiverse areas in the world outside of the tropics. The Big Thicket contains over 100 species of trees and shrubs, inclusive of stands of mature bald cypress and water tupelo, the dominant tree species of the swamp. The remaining dark swamp, piney meadows, and acid bogs provide habitat for thousands of species of flowering plants, mammals, birds, 60 reptiles, and amphibians. In

a 1970s oral history of the Big Thicket, Judge Andrew Leak Bevil, one of the swamp's notable hog raisers and bear hunter extraordinaire, observed: "The leaves have fallen on these hummocks for thousands and thousands of years and that ground is a natural loam that will grow anything."

At the western edge of the Big Thicket the subtropical jungle makes way for Houston, the fourth most populous city in the United States. Briefly the capital of the Republic of Texas, Houston was designed to be a commercial hub perfectly located at a natural turning basin** at confluence of the Buffalo Bayou and the White Oak Bayou. Much of the city is located on the gulf coastal plain, and its vegetation is classified as Western Gulf coastal grasslands.

Having been born on the bayou, flooding has plagued the city of Houston since its inception. The native flora of East Texas, better adjusted to persistent high water than its bipedal inhabitants, has enabled Houston to maintain an impressive urban forest. Urban forests offer a wide range of environmental benefits, such as stormwater management, air pollution mitigation, reduced air temperatures, wildlife habitat, and aesthetic appeal.

In 2015, the Forest Inventory and Analysis division of the US Forest Service and the agricultural staff of Texas A&M studied and inventoried Houston's trees. The study indicated that Houston has about 33.3 million trees, representing more than 63 species, providing a canopy cover of 18.4%. In a city notorious for rain, heat, and humidity (and often all three at once), shade is a highly coveted, heat-reprieving resource for all Houstonians. Not surprisingly, the study showed that the species of trees with the most environmental importance to Houston

---

* The fire was ordered set by Confederate Captain James Kaiser.
** A turning basin is a wider body of water that allows a ship to turn and reverse direction.

were all native, in particular the yaupon holly, southern live oak, sugarberry, and loblolly pine.

Floods

Today, as a result of Houston's rapid and poorly planned expansion over a low-lying swamp, the city is faced with a persistent existential threat, that of flooding. Houston is relatively flat, about 50 feet above sea level, and, given that there is only a 4-foot range between the highest and lowest parts of the city, flooding is a recurring problem. The suburbs on the seaward side are even lower, about 40 feet above sea level. When it rains the water cannot easily find its way to the sea and takes a long time to drain.

On undeveloped land, precipitation infiltrates into the ground and slowly recharges underground aquifers or moves laterally to recharge streams, lakes, and wetlands. By contrast, developed sites produce dramatically more surface runoff due to impervious surfaces and soil compaction. As a consequence, pollutants in stormwater are flushed downstream and the pulsating flows of the runoff contribute to increased flooding of the urban area as well as the destabilization of the downstream channel systems.

Proposals are in place to raise Houston's foundations 2 feet above the 500-year floodplain* and drill massive stormwater tunnels 100 to 200 feet below the ground to channel water directly toward the Gulf of Mexico through a system of pumps. It all sounds risky, given the seas may well rise before Houston can. In the near term, homeowners with property in a flood zone must become familiar with how water flows around their property and do their best to redirect the deluges when they come, while their newly planted trees and shrubs take root. They will eventually drain stormwater more efficiently, impede rising tides, and prevent soil erosion. However, in the longer-term battle for Houston and the like, water will increasingly gain advantage as temperatures rise.

Big Thicket Wildlife

Piglet: "It's a little Anxious," he said to himself, "to be a Very Small Animal Entirely surrounded by water."** Razorback boars in the Big Thicket, Piglet's invasive feral cousins, have no such qualms. The Big Thicket is bayou country, complete with alligators, turtles, and water snakes, but it also has drier pockets, with ranging coyotes and dawdling armadillos. The Big Thicket is the meeting place between the easternmost extension of America's prairies and the westernmost extension of its woodlands. It is also a meeting place between the wildlife of temperate and subtropical climate zones, as well as wildlife from salt and freshwater zones.

Two of the greatest avian migration routes, the Mississippi Flyway and the Southern Flyway, intersect in the air space above the Big Thicket, making it a melting pot of birds, especially during the migration periods, when several hundred species of migrating birds join more than 300 resident species. The Big Thicket is the last retreat for several rare birds, such as Swanson's warbler and the red-cockaded woodpecker. The ivory-billed woodpecker, recently written off as America's latest extinction, has again been spotted in the Big Thicket. Both the jaguarundi and red wolf are making their last ditch stands deep in the Thicket's densest woods.

---

*   The concept of floodplains entails a convoluted statistical analysis of the probability of floods.
**   *Winnie-the-Pooh* (1926), A. A. Milne.

WEST: CENTRAL VALLEY (SACRAMENTO, CALIFORNIA)

California can be divided into four distinct ecoregions, each of which contains unique ecological communities of plants and animals. These ecoregions are grouped into the following climatic zones: Desert, Mediterranean, Forested Mountains, and Coastal Forests. The Central Valley is a long, flat valley that traverses the interior of California, 40 to 60 miles wide, approximately 450 miles long, and runs north-northeast to south-southeast inland parallel to the Pacific coast. It is bounded in the east by the Sierra Nevada Mountains and to the west by the Coastal Ranges. The northern portion of the Central Valley is located in the Mediterranean zone and the southern portion is in the Desert zone. The pre-Columbian nomadic bands that roamed the northern Valley were gentler on the land than their brethren to the east. Neither their lighting of small brush fires, over-gathering of plentiful acorns, or modest hunting techniques left a lasting mark on the Valley's immense tracts of riparian forest and savannah lands.

Evolution of California—Central Valley

In 1808, Gabriel Moraga, a Spanish military officer and explorer, turned inland from the Bay of San Francisco, passed the coastal mountains, and discovered the great Central Valley that lay beyond. He named its major river *Sacramento*, for the Most Holy Sacrament of the Catholic Eucharist, and brought the Anthropocene maelstrom into the Central Valley. At that time, the northern portion of the Valley was endowed with a natural environment the scope and magnitude of which is difficult to fully comprehend today. Two major river systems, the Sacramento and the San Joaquin, drained the valley. Flooding in winter and spring, these rivers and

their tributaries formed vast flood basins and huge seasonal lakes. Lush marsh vegetation occupied the wetter sites. Extensive perennial grassland and scattered oak woodlands were found on the drier uplands. Vast strips of dense forest cut through the vegetation communities hugging the rivers and stream systems. These riparian forests developed on rich deposits of silt that lined most of the Valley's natural drainage systems.

Until gold was discovered there in 1848, the same year the United States ended the Mexican-American War and annexed the entire Southwest, Alta California was an obscure and unprofitable province. Within 2 years the area was so overrun by gold-seekers, they came to be

known as forty-niners. The effects of the gold rush on the Central Valley's indigenous populations were substantial; whole tribal societies were attacked and pushed off their lands while entire ecologies were razed for farmland. The remaining riparian forests, often the only significant woody vegetation on the valley floor, were quickly consumed by farmers who needed timber for building houses, fences, and fuel. Steamships that began to ply the Sacramento River were also heavy users of local wood for fuel. As early as 1868, the general scarcity of woody vegetation became apparent. The pressure on the land increased when the farmers found that the soil on the river's natural levees was highly fertile, easily managed, and not subject to the seasonal flooding of nearby lower-lying ground.

Water, too, became a problem as agriculture expanded in the Central Valley, and the demand began to exceed the supply. A problem particular to farming in the Central Valley was that there was too much water in spring and winter and not enough water in summer. In an attempt to resolve what remains an insolvable problem, water development and reclamation projects were haphazardly initiated, further degrading the Valley's native wetland systems. Parallel with the rampant expansion of agriculture, cities grew in number and size, built upon flood basins or in active floodplains. The Central Valley was the ocean floor some eons ago, and when the coastal mountains rose before it, the only outlet for high waters was the Sacramento River. And, given that the Sacramento River is a mere 10 feet above sea level at Sacramento and the San Francisco Bay is 100 miles distant, it takes a long time for the valley to drain. In times of flooding, the Central Valley is like a gigantic clogged sink.

In response to constant flooding, levees were constructed around the city of Sacramento. Soon after, vast projects were commenced to reclaim the surrounding marshlands and floodplains of the Central Valley. In 1868, William Green, Sacramento's fervid advocate of irrigation, promoted legislation that freed reclamation projects from the most basic environmental controls, resulting in the destruction of the majority of the Valley's remaining riparian forests. Since then, numerous and controversial water projects have been the hallmark of Central Valley development. The demand for water for the urban, commercial, and agricultural development of the Valley has been directly or indirectly responsible for the degradation of the last of its forests. While there is a growing appreciation for the value of the remnants of these forests, as they continue to provide habitat for the wildlife, they have lost all semblance of their original state.

Sacramento was initially called the City of the Plains because the early settlers had so utterly devoured what timber was available. But this changed after a gold miner planted cottonwood trees near his tent and the fad caught on.* By the 1930s, Sacramento was being called the City of Trees and, given the fertility of the floodplain underlying the city, it has grown into one of the more robust urban forests in the United States.

Central Valley's Wildlife

In the not-so-distant past, California was home to tens of millions of migrating ducks and geese that overwintered in the Central Valley's wetlands. As the wetlands disappeared, farmers and hunters waged an all-out—no holds barred, no quarter given—war on waterfowl. As late as the 1940s and 1950s, the war raged on. "No attempt should be made to belittle the supreme contempt with which a duck's life is considered in Colusa and adjacent counties," wrote one Fish & Wildlife Service official.** Today, 95% of these wetlands are gone. What remains only exists on a few small refuges that cannot provide enough food to support the few million waterfowl survivors that still winter in the Central Valley. But a truce has been declared. Each evening after sundown at the Sacramento National Wildlife Refuge, hundreds of thousands of waterfowl fly off from the refuge's sanctuary into the surrounding rice fields, where standing water and stands of rice are purposely left after the harvest for environmental purposes. These waterfowl eat rice all night long and then, just before sunrise, return to the safety of the sanctuary's wetlands. The waterfowl's fly-off is a poignant illustration of how farmers and conservationists can come together to support a significant population of birds each winter. As long as enough people and groups can come together to provide water and habitat, and as long as links between habitats are not broken, what wildlife that still remains has a chance to adapt.

---

*   *From Nature to Nurture: The History of Sacramento's Urban Forest* (1998), E. Gregory McPherson and Nina Luttinger.
**   "The Duck Problem" (1944), E.E. Horn (Records of the Bureau of Sport Fisheries and Wildlife).

NORTHWEST: PUGET SOUND
(OLYMPIA, WASHINGTON)

Dominated by Douglas fir and hemlock, the conifer forests of the Pacific Northwest ecosystem are full of large, old trees. They began their domination of the landscape about 10,000 years ago when the glaciers that covered Puget Sound receded from a warming continent. Ponderosa pine, noble fir, western hemlock, and lodgepole pine became common at high elevations, Sitka spruce along the Pacific coast, extending north all the way to Vancouver Island. Fossils suggest that in this previous, warm period, fires were frequent. Today's cooler, wetter period started about 3,500 years ago, around the time native tribes and affiliations established themselves along the coast. These tribes shared a common language, traditions, practices, and the centrality of salmon as a resource. Trading for services and material goods became a vital component of tribal life on the Northwest Coast.

Evolution of Puget Sound

The native vegetation of the Pacific Northwest has accidentally and deliberately been modified over generations of coastal communities setting fires around Puget Sound to attract browsing animals. When the Europeans arrived in the last decades of the 18th century, they found indigenous peoples hunting deer and elk in fields of bracken, camas, and huckleberry. They also found common ground, for a short time, with the trade-oriented tribes. They had brought with them new species like sheep, cattle, cheat grass, wheat, and potatoes, and they quickly learned to set fires to create grazable land. Forests became overwhelmed by too many fires set before they could recover.

Puget Sound's forests occupy a north-south depression between the Olympia Peninsula and western slopes of the Cascade Mountains, extending from just below the Canadian border to the lower Columbia River just above the Oregon border. Relief in the valley is moderate, with elevations ranging from sea level to 1,400 feet. This ecoregion lies within Washington State's most populated areas and encompasses the cities of Bellingham, Seattle, Tacoma, and Olympia. As a direct consequence of this urban growth, only 5% the region's original habitat remains, and most of these remaining areas have been heavily altered. What remains are disturbed and isolated islands of old-growth forests, bogs, and prairie-oak woodlands, hedged in by urbanization and agriculture.

Surprisingly, little is known with certainty

about the presettlement forests around Puget Sound; no direct scientific description was undertaken before the original forests were thoroughly cut over. By 1960, industrial forestry had consumed almost all the coastal forests, as well as those in the lowlands and into the flanking foothills. What little can be learned about this forest was recorded in the mid-19th century, when the US General Land Office (GLO) surveyed this region as a precondition to opening it up to settlement. The GLO used natural trees to witness their survey's compass quadrant grid lines, quarter corners, and corners. The GLO instructed the various townships to use whichever four trees happened to lie close to the nearest reference post, which would disintegrate over time, a practice that resulted in 24 witness trees per quadrant. Each recorded tree was identified by its common name, diameter, and location to the post. These records were dutifully kept, and a study of them reveals much about the presettlement forests.

The GLO's witness tree study shows that conifers vastly outnumbered hardwoods; one-third of all trees were Douglas fir, and the balance was mostly western red cedar and western hemlock. In all instances, just a few trees were exceptionally large, notably the red cedar, at 15 feet in diameter, and the Douglas fir, up to 8 feet in diameter. The study also shows that, contrary to popular belief, the trees of the presettlement forests were not uniformly of immense girth and height. That western firs, cedars, and hemlocks attain very large heights and widths should not be construed as evidence that presettlement forests were primarily filled with gigantic ancient trees.

Industrial logging was not always seen for what it is: the wanton destruction of the environment and the disenfranchisement of the indigenous peoples who depended upon the for-

ests for survival. By the mid-1800s, the state of Washington existed to supply timber to California's precipitous increase in population following the Gold Rush. Clear cutting was deemed a necessary step in taming the land for the new inhabitants as well as ensuring the departure of its first inhabitants. In 1887, the Northern Pacific railroad opened a direct rail link over the Cascade Mountains to Tacoma. With the forests of Wisconsin, Missouri, and Minnesota already grossly depleted, and the railroad at their disposal, Washington quickly assumed the role of the primary timber supplier to the nation. After the World War II, with private supplies of trees in decline, lumber companies became more dependent on Washington's national forests, and the forest services were happy to give it to them. During the 1960s and 1970s, the forest management services continually increased the annual allowable cut, with the result that the timber harvest on federal lands reached an all-time high in 1987.

But the times were changing. Before World War II, only a small percentage of Americans were conservationists. After the war, the situation changed as the average person's income increased and, as more leisure time was available, the popularity of hiking, camping, fishing, and other types of outdoor recreation skyrocketed. As a result of increased outdoor experiences, more Americans became interested in preserving forests for recreation. By the mid-1960s, a powerful environmental movement began to emerge. The passage of the Endangered Species Act (ESA), in 1973, was the first major victory for the environmentalists. The ESA recognized that all native species were vital members of a larger ecosystem worthy of protection and required the US Fish & Wildlife Service to not only identify threatened plants and animals but also to take action to promote the recovery of these species.

Toward the close of the 20th century, total deforestation tactics had been replaced by selective harvesting of mature trees. However, the war between the environmentalists and the lumber industry continued until the control of Washington's old-growth forests was decided by one of its more venerable inhabitants, the northern spotted owl. When the ESA declared the northern spotted owl a protected species, logging in national forests was brought to a screeching, or perhaps hooting, halt, and the battle was joined. The controversy pitted loggers and sawmill owners against environmentalists. In support of loggers, bumper stickers appeared reading: *Kill a Spotted Owl, Save a Logger*, or *I Like Spotted Owls, Fried*.

The environmentalists retaliated by declaring the spotted owl an indicator species whose role, similar to that of canaries in coal mines, was to provide protection for the entire ecosystem. In the end, the spotted owl emerged victorious, logging jobs were lost, and the war was over.

Northwest Washington, despite the constant predation and mismanagement of its natural resources, is still one of the most ecologically diverse areas in the nation and contains some of America's most productive forests. The Puget Sound Lowland region is a centerpiece of that diversity and productivity. While the management challenges resulting from post-European settlement and modification of the natural landscape are nearly insurmountable, the leftover mosaic of forest and vegetative communities in this region is worth saving; its distinctive features are unique products of the region's glacial history and linkages to marine waters.

Puget Sound's Wildlife

While Puget Sound's mammalian marine wildlife—whales, orcas, otters, seals—get all the attention, its native bumblebees are the ecosystem's true but little heroes. About 85% of the world's flowering plants depend upon pollination from wildlife, and bumblebees make up one of the most important groups of pollinators. Plants and bees have evolved together, shaping ecosystems. For example, different species of bumblebees have different length tongues, each suited to pollinating different plants. For the past decade, Washington's biologists have reported a sharp decline in the bumblebee populations due to loss of habitat, and at least four species of Washington's bumblebees risk extinction. Besides loss of habitat, another problem facing bumblebees is a loss of genetic diversity, which can also lead to extinction. To sustain diversity, these bees need to connect with other colonies of their kind, something that is increasingly difficult in the Puget Sound lowlands as suburbia encroaches upon and fragments the native habitat. Bumblebees live in modest underground burrows, often situated near the plants they fertilize, and their proximity threatens no one with stings. The best way to help bumblebees is to provide them with a new bee-friendly habitat that also allows them to connect with colonies of similar species.

CHAPTER 3

Understanding Suburban Landscaping

"'I want to get the grass cut,' he said. We both looked at the grass—there was a sharp line where my ragged lawn ended and the darker, well-kept expanse of his began. I suspected that he meant my grass. . . . At eleven o'clock a man in a raincoat, dragging a lawnmower, tapped at my front door and said that Mr. Gatsby had sent him over to cut my grass."
—*The Great Gatsby* (1925), F. Scott Fitzgerald

THE OPEN GRASS communal landscape is America's democratic rebuttal to Europe's walled and hedged-in homes. Traditional suburban landscaping, where the house is the centerpiece of a well-kept lawn, has long promoted this social order. But once the homeowner has come to accept that a turf-grass lawn is, in a deep sense, unethical, the high ground looms and the grass must go. A sylvan landscape does not seek to disrupt this grass-bound unity but rather promotes a means of eliminating the turf grass and replacing it with a generous profusion of native trees, shrubs, and ground covers. However, it is not sufficient that the resulting landscape simply enhances the environment; it must also beautify the neighborhood, support the environment, and soothe the social soul. To achieve such a fair objective, while at the same time cutting ties with the swathe of communal turf grass, a sylvan landscape must be designed so that it is appealing to those who are looking in, as well as to those who are looking out.

THE DIALECTIC OF SUBURBIA

Turf grass became comfortable to suburbanites, profitable for the yard maintenance industry, and controlled by a despotic municipal force. In step with municipal codes have come lawn patrols to maintain order in the turf. Eagle-eyed persons have set themselves to the task of patrolling the streets and taking umbrage against those whose lawns fail to meet community standards, and the immoderate virtues of conservatives are to be feared far more than their petty vices. These vigilantes have the power to first annoy, then to cite, and finally to initiate legal proceedings against those whom they perceive as guilty of weed trespass. Such are the forces of political ecology at work, shaping the environment by setting standards.

Political ecologist Paul Robbins, for his book, *Lawn People* (2007), subtitled "How Grass, Weeds, and Chemicals Make Us Who We Are," interviewed hundreds of people about their

"Florida Scrub Jay"

lawns. Many of the interviewees stated that if their grass grew too high, neighbors would come by and ask them if their lawnmower was broken. Others said that neighbors came by when they were out of town and mowed their lawns for them.

Today, the need for water conservation has become a sensitive item in many municipalities where water for irrigating lawns or washing cars has been strictly regulated. Plants that grow wild in their native region have evolved over untold millennia and have established a self-regulating ecosystem that requires no more water than is provided by the normal precipitation. Already, in the drier regions, state and local authorities have begun to encourage suburbanites to replace as much turf grass as possible with plants that do not require irrigation, or even lay down gravel and rocks in their stead. The importance of saving water can only gain momentum, and the suburbanite who replaces turf grass with native trees, shrubs, and ground cover cannot only anticipate a favorable soft-

ening of the lawn codes but also an increase in property value as the trees mature. For those who remain faithful to yesterday's idols, brown may well become the new green.

PROPERTY MAINTENANCE CODES

Before delving into the modalities of designing a sylvan landscape, there are pitfalls in both state and municipal property maintenance codes that need to be understood and accommodated rather than ignored or haphazardly circumnavigated. For once the concept of grass lawns took root, the fact that anyone *could* keep up a lawn swiftly transmuted into the notion that everyone *ought* to. In step with this transformation, townships and municipalities around the country adopted weed laws mandating that all yards, the front yard in particular, be maintained to a certain uniform standard. Despite the fact that it is now an accepted truth that a pesticide-laden lawn destroys the environment, almost all of the old weed laws remain on the books. Nor has the new awareness of global warming, climate change, or water shortages moved the municipalities to review their codes or caused the pro-lawn associations to recant past sins. Instead, the pro-lawn forces, taking a stance akin to that taken by Big Tobacco when it set out to prove that smoking did not cause cancer, have redoubled their efforts to try to convince the public that turf-grass lawns are beneficial to the environment.

Given that a property without turf grass is somewhat of an anomaly in suburban lands, it is best that homeowners, before embarking on a sylvan landscape design, understand how the yard codes could affect their design and their choice of plants, ground covers in particular. While these codes can range from the general to the doggedly specific, they usually contain the following strictures: the heights of grass or weeds—the distinction is rarely clear—should not exceed 8 or 10 inches; the trees, hedges, and shrubs that lie close to the sidewalk or street must not impede vehicular or pedestrian traffic; and the cultivation of noxious weeds or invasive plants is prohibited.* While these codes seem to take turf-grass lawns for granted, they do not mandate which type of low-growing plant could replace turf grass, nor do they limit the number of trees and shrubs the yard could contain, and therein lies the design solution. HOAs (homeowners associations), another thorn in the crown of turf grass, may impose further rules about the extent to which the grass lawn can be replaced, particularly the front lawn. But nature offers remedies for almost any definition of grass, and here is where America's rich diversity of native species of herbaceous plants that can be used as ground cover comes into play.

In essence, a homeowner who understands the relevant codes can design the placement and choose the species of ground cover with an eye to avoid offending any of the lawn and order powers. A few examples of relevant sections of municipal and state codes will help to illustrate the nature and reach of most:

East Syracuse, New York

Regarding the upkeep of the lawn and weeds on the exterior of your property, there are two codes that must be followed within the Village of East Syracuse. One is the International Property Maintenance Code adopted by the State of New York; the other is our own local law within our Village Municipal Code.

§ 744.0 Weeds: No owner or occupant shall allow vegetation other than trees and shrubbery to grow higher than 8 inches in any yard that abuts a public thoroughfare or in a street margin abutting their property.

§ 302.4 Weeds: All immediate exterior property shall be maintained free from weeds or plant growth in excess of 10 inches. All noxious weeds shall be prohibited. Weeds shall be defined as all grasses, annual plants, and vegetation, other than trees or shrubs provided; however, this term shall not include cultivated flowers and gardens.

Roanoke, Virginia

§ 33-17 Definitions: (g) Weed or weeds mean any plant, grass or other vegetation over ten (10) inches in height growing upon a parcel in the City of Roanoke, including, but not limited to, any sage brush, poison oak, poison ivy, tree of heaven (or paradise tree), ragweed, dandelions, milkweed, Canada thistle, and any other undesirable growth, excluding trees, orna-

---

* Unsurprisingly, almost all plants categorized as noxious or invasive are not native to the United States.

mental shrubbery, vegetable and flower gardens purposefully planted and maintained by the property owner or occupant free of weed hazard or nuisance, cultivated crops, or undisturbed woodland not otherwise in violation.

§ 33-18: Weeds and trash declared public nuisance; abatement required. Weeds growing or trash lying on any parcel shall constitute a public nuisance, except that in the case of a parcel greater than 1 acre in an area of natural vegetation growing more than 50 feet from every property line shall not constitute a public nuisance. It shall be unlawful to cause or allow a public nuisance with respect to any parcel. The owner of any parcel shall abate any public nuisance with respect to his parcel.

Minnesota Dept. of Agriculture

§ 18.75-18.91: defines a noxious weed as an annual, biennial, or perennial plant that the Commissioner of Agriculture designates to be injurious to public health, the environment, public roads, crops, livestock, or other property. The purpose of the law is to protect residents of the state from the injurious effects of noxious weeds. There are currently 42 plant species regulated as noxious weeds in Minnesota. Twenty-three plants are listed as Prohibited Noxious Weeds, which consist of two regulatory lists: 14 plants listed on the Prohibited Eradicate List and 9 plants listed on the Prohibited Control List. Fifteen species are listed as Restricted Noxious Weeds and four species are listed as a Specially Regulated Plants that can be enforced under specific conditions. Property maintenance codes tend to be front-yard specific. Besides limiting the heights of grass and the rights of passage, these codes can also include rules for trimming of trees leaning over a property's boundary lines, the removal of debris, and whatever else goes against the common grain. Otherwise, the care of the backyard

is pretty much left to the homeowner's discretion, with the possible exceptions of husbanding barnyard fowl, harboring beasts of a less than domestic character, and the stockpiling of foul-smelling items. This last restriction can include compost, given that bushels of cut grass laden with pesticides and mixed with kitchen refuse can create an odoriferous slime. On the other hand, compost solely derived from the detritus of a sylvan landscape is not malodorous and, given a year or so to decompose, becomes the perfect fertilizer. Natural compost is a strong element that will maintain the fertility of the soil and the health of the plants, and care should be taken to see exactly which composting methods are forbidden by code to better learn which best methods could be permitted. With the sad exception of milkweed (to be discussed below), all state and municipal maintenance codes allow any plant native to a region to grow and prosper in that region's suburbs.

THE HIGH GROUND

The progress of human civilization has degraded the environment, adversely affected the climate, and caused the extinction of countless species of life, both plant and animal. Those who would wish to reverse the degradation of their environment must be attentive to mending their own ways while helping others repair whatever damage is repairable. But how can this be done? Despite the progress of science and religion, the true path to environmental salvation has yet to be revealed, and many questions about nature's systems and man's impact upon these systems have yet to be answered. Yet the path forward, even if fraught with uncertainty, would seem to be lined with native plants.

If choosing the right native plant is essential to the success of a sylvan landscape, then a study of botany suggests itself. But a study of botany is too vast a subject for the one-time practitioner. A more sensible course of study would be to research a particular state's native plant database* and form an idea of what is available. Afterward, a walk through a reasonably intact forest would acquaint the homeowner with what actually thrives in the here and now.

The trees and shrubs in such a local forest, given that the forest has had a reasonable length to time to grow and prosper, will have formed themselves into harmonious groups in accordance with environmental differences. If some clearings in the forest, whether caused by natural or human disturbance, appear more harmonious and beautiful than others, it is because nature has had sufficient time to repair herself. By paying particular attention to these clearings and to openings at the forest's edges, ideas can form for the design of a sylvan landscape. In such clearings the understory plants, or the smaller trees and larger shrubs, are given the extra sunlight afforded by the clearing to come into their own. All of these understory plants will likely be natives, albeit there could be an invasive species running amok somewhere. Absent the invasive species, such a forest opening could be replicated on a suburban property.

THE EDGE EFFECT

Edges arrive when two or more contrasting habitat types come into contact with each other. The changes in species abundance and community structure in the space between these contrasting habitats are often termed "edge effects." Rye worldwide effects of edge differ, whereas those in North America, where the forest meets the plain in a slow natural way rather than with an abrupt change, usually results in a greater diversity of plants and an increase of wildlife species,

birds in particular. More abrupt changes, on the contrary, present less species exchange between habitats and a higher flow of physical variables, which is detrimental to species ability.

Although edge effect is usually analyzed over a far broader area than a suburban yard, many of its concepts apply to smaller projects as well, particularly the suitability of human-modified habitats for native species and the response of these species to habitat edges. In natural settings, the larger trees of the forest give way to smaller understory trees, then shrubs, and finally to grasses and wildflowers. This rich middle space—the edge—is attractive to both the wildlife of the forest and the wildlife of the plains. In settings where the change in habitat is more abrupt, the larger trees end where the meadow begins, and there is less biodiversity at the edge. Suburban housing developments, ripped out of the forests or meadows at the outskirts of cites, are abrupt disturbances, similar to the construction of a highway or a forest fire, and a main cause of species extinction.

PLANT KINGDOM BASICS

The plant kingdom revolves around predominantly photosynthetic organisms, meaning those that transform water, carbon dioxide, and sunlight into oxygen and sugar. Plants such as trees, shrubs, and ground covers can be deciduous or evergreen, depending on whether or not they keep their leaves over winter. Flowers can be annual or perennial, depending on whether they wither and die at the end of the year or live on to the next. To further clarify their physical characteristics:

Trees
Trees, the largest of living things, have a tremendous ecological impact on the environ-

---

*   Every state in the Union seems to have at least one such database, sometimes a dozen.

ment: their canopies will dictate the nature of the understory and herbaceous layers. Trees emit oxygen, store carbon, stabilize the soil, filter water, release water, and provide habitat for wildlife. For the homeowner, they provide shade, natural air conditioning, sound blocking, and less dust. For the community, they reduce surface runoff water and filter pollen and smoke from the air.

When a particular species of tree evolves in a specific region and creates its own ecosystem, it receives the title of foundational species. Oak trees, for example, were once a foundational species in the east-central United States before logging took its toll. Oak trees supported a plethora of wildlife, this in part to their open canopy structure, which created bright conditions in understories and led to greater species-richness on the ground. The American chestnut tree, also an important foundational tree in the eastern forests, was nearly wiped out by an invasive pathogen of European origin.[*]

Trees most conspicuously found within a particular ecosystem are given the title of dominant species. A difficulty in defining dominant tree communities is that they can operate on a time scale measured in centuries, and many forests are in a state of transition from one set of dominant species to another. Maple trees, for example, are a species that became dominant

[*] The American Chestnut Foundation has helped to reverse this catastrophic loss.

Hartford in October
View A

in the northeastern United States after the oak and hemlock populations declined. Dominant species of trees provide the greatest biomass in any forest and shelter and feed the greatest number and variety of wildlife, again ensuring species-richness on the ground.

Trees that are the first to colonize previously disrupted or damaged ecosystems receive the title of pioneer species. Pioneer trees—cedars and willows, for example—begin a chain of ecological succession that ultimately leads to a biodiverse-steady state ecosystem. Given that uncolonized land may have poor-quality soil with few nutrients, pioneer species have to be hardy and often have adaptations to adverse conditions, such as long roots, root nodes containing nitrogen-fixing bacteria, and a tendency to reproduce asexually—traits that allow pioneer trees to survive where other types could not.

Due to their biological diversity, it is hard to accurately categorize trees, but heights, growth rate, texture, and shape are helpful common denominators:

HEIGHT: Trees are often referred to by their size, specifically their height at maturity, and are divided into the following categories: very small—less than 15 feet, small—15 to 25 feet, medium-sized—25 to 50 feet, large—50 to 80 feet, and very large—80 feet and up.

GROWTH RATE: Growth rates refer to a tree's annual vertical increase in height, which is influenced by variables such as climate, soil, water, and light. Growth rates are usually divided into the following categories: slow—growth of 12 inches or less per year, moderate—growth of 13 to 24 inches per year, and fast—growth of 25 inches or more per year. In every year, every part of a tree will expand in girth and in length from its trunk to its roots and the tips of the twigs.

TEXTURE: The texture of a tree is determined by the density and sizes of its twigs, stems, and leaves. Textural qualities control the degree of shade each tree throws: coarse borders on the opaque, medium allows some light penetration, and fine can be seen through.

SHAPE: The directions in which the branches of a tree grow, whether shaped by nature or to be dictated by pruning, determine the tree's shape. The round, vase, weeping, and irregularly shaped trees often provide the most visual interest, whereas cone- and columnar-shaped trees are often chosen for utilitarian purposes, such as wind breaks or delineating property lines.

The full outward diameter of a tree's crown is called its canopy. The outline of the canopy projected onto the ground is called the drip line, and, as anyone who has stood under a tree when it rains can tell you, this is where most of the rainfall drips off the leaves.

The multitude of variables that influence a tree's growth makes estimating tree heights, shapes, and canopy sizes after 5, 10, or 20 years an approximate exercise at best. However, regardless of its age, there is a reasonable way to determine a tree's maturity. Almost every species of tree goes through the same stages: infancy—it is small, thin, and vulnerable; youth—it has long slender branches and a pointed top, a stage at which a tree's growth and form can be influenced by careful pruning; prime—it has a full, round-topped crown filled with long, strong branches; middle-age—its crown flattens out and its limbs grow thicker and heavier; senior—it has a flat-topped canopy of heavy limbs with gaps appearing in the canopy as major limb systems start dying out; twilight—its larger limbs die and break off, leaving a small crown of scattered large limbs and short twigs; and death—all trees, which are the longest living of all living things, inevitably die at some point, falling and decaying back into the soil. Whether this process takes 50, 200, or 1,000 years to complete, the transitional stages remain the same.

Shrubs

Shrubs are loosely defined as perennial woody plants that branch into multiple stems at the base, are relatively leafy, and are smaller than small trees. Other definitions characterize shrubs as possessing multiple stems with no main trunk. These definitions are not reliable, however, for there are some shrubs, such as lilacs and honeysuckle, that, under especially favorable environmental conditions, grow to the size of small trees. Further confusing the issue, and without delving into the oriental art of bonsai, where a specialist can keep a large tree pruned down to the size of a small umbrella, some species of shrubs can be pruned up to the size of trees, just as some trees can be pruned down to the size of shrubs.

As plants of smaller stature than trees, shrubs often occupy a mid-story habitat and have a significant, beneficial influence on the presence of insects, particularly pollinators, and on attracting both nesting and migratory birds. While there is no clear horticultural difference between the usage of the terms "shrub" and "bush," shrubs are generally understood to be plants that are cultivated, are shaped in garden settings, and typically have vertical foliage that does not touch the ground. Bushes are whatever grows in the wild that is smaller than a tree and not a species of ground cover. Shrub sizes are often determined by the optimal height to which they can be maintained: small shrubs at around 3 feet or less, medium-sized shrubs between 3 and 6 feet, and large shrubs between 6 and 12 feet. Like trees, shrubs can

be evergreen or deciduous and have broadleaf or needled foliage. Much like trees, shrubs prevent runoff water and soil erosion, playing an important role in ecosystems. Shrubs are nutritionally diverse plants and bear various combinations of flowers, nuts, fruits, cones, berries, drupes, and seeds.

Ground Covers

In a natural ecosystem, ground cover refers to any type of low-growing herbaceous plant that lacks woody stems and constitutes the layer that lies below the shrub level. Common examples of ground covers are bulbs, grasses, sedges, rushes, and ferns. Ground covers can spread by a rhizome, a continually growing horizontal root; a stolon, a horizontal plant runner; or offsets and tip layering, both of which involve horizontal stems, bending into the ground. Plants used as ground cover for landscaping are typically short, rapid-growing perennials that do not require a lot of soil. Besides being attractive and essential to the health of the ecosystem, ground cover protects the topsoil from erosion and drought. Ideally, any native ground cover chosen for landscaping will develop rapidly and become sufficiently dense to inhibit competition from weeds.

Ground covers are often overlooked in eco-

"Texas Frogfruit"

logical analyses because they contribute the smallest amount of the environment's biomass. However, ground cover is crucial to the survival of many environments. In a forest, ground cover can contribute up to 90% of the ecosystem's plant diversity. Ground cover also promotes the development of desirable microbial and invertebrate population; its vegetation breaks the force of water droplets that would otherwise destroy the soil's structure.

Wildflowers

Wildflowers are an attractive and useful species of ground cover; there are more than 6,000 species native to the United States, each one perfectly adapted to its region's climate and beautiful to the eye of the beholder. Wildflowers are a key element in the herbaceous layer and are essentially low-growing, flowering plants that thrive in the wild without cultivation. The leaves and seeds of wildflowers provide food for wildlife, and their flowers provide nectar and pollen to insects as well as smaller species of birds. Planted en masse, wildflowers provide space for the smaller wildlife to nest and breed.

Wildflowers can be annuals, which bloom quickly from seed and then die after they have dropped their own seeds; or they can be perennials, which do not bloom until their second year and then return every year from the same roots. A word of perennial caution: some species tend to clump and must be thinned out and/or divided periodically.

Wildflowers are usually planted from seeds, and packages of wildflower seeds are readily available. However, and this is very important, wildflower seeds should only be purchased from a reliable source. Wildflower seeds can be planted, or rather sown, in spring for summer flowers or sown in fall for spring flowers. The trick is to sow them on a sunny patch of prepared soil, after which these hardy natives will take care of themselves as well as the visiting pollinators. Wildflowers are easy to refresh or renew, it just takes a few handfuls of seed.

There are more than 100 species of milkweeds and all are true wildflowers, not weeds as their name suggests. Milkweeds deserve special attention, as they are essential for the survival of the butterfly as well as being beneficial to a host of other pollinators. Monarch caterpillars can only eat milkweed. If a monarch butterfly lays its eggs on any other plant than a milkweed, when its eggs hatch and caterpillars emerge, they cannot eat and will ultimately starve to death. Reversing their previous anti-milkweed policies, the US Fish & Wildlife Service has now launched programs that encourage suburbanites to plant milkweed in their yards, hopefully keeping the monarch butterfly from becoming extinct.

"Monarch butterfly"

BOTANICAL CAVEATS

Scientific Names

Part of the botanical learning curve involves dealing with the quasi-Latin scientific names of plants. Latin, beginning with the fall of the Roman Empire in the west and ending with the fall of the British Empire in the east, was the international language for communicating philosophical works. This singular anomaly results from the Catholic Church's steadfast determination to keep the bible in Latin. While the Church's motives were not entirely pure, the Latin language does have inherent advantages for the taxon-minded because, like its bellicose creators, it is a very efficient language with few idiosyncrasies. In 1753, the Swedish biologist Carl Linnaeus, coeval with the rise of the British colonial tide, writing in Latin and styling himself Carolus Linnaeus, formalized the binomial Latin system for classifying plants and animals that is still used today.[*]

The first part of a species Latin name, the genus name, is a proper noun so it is capitalized, and the second part is an epithet and not capitalized. As an example, *Quercus* is the Latin word for an oak tree, *alba* is the Latin word for white, and *Quercus alba* refers to the white oak tree. Linnaeus' reason for writing in Latin was irreproachable; a dead language did not favor any living language and certainly was more understandable than his native Swedish. Unfortunately, there were not nearly enough Latin nouns to describe the vast taxa of life discovered after the fall of Rome. After Linnaeus ran out of authentic Latin nouns, he turned to the Greek language. After the scientific community had exhausted Greek, they began inventing Latinized names. For example, a newly discovered species of a nearly blind serpentine amphibian that buries its head in the sand if threatened was given the scientific name *Dermorphis donaldtrumpi*,[**] hardly a Latin formulation, but rather one that speaks to the amphibian's habits. But for whatever their origin, scientific names are unique, and given that different plants can have the same local name, it is advisable to use its scientific name when ordering.

Cultivars

In antiquity, the word "cultivar" originated from the need to distinguish between wild plants and those with characteristics that arose in cultivation. Today's definition is more precise, as an industry has grown up around the fabrication of cultivars: A cultivar is an assemblage of plants that: (a) has been selected for a particular character or combination of characters, (b) is distinct, uniform, and stable in those characters, and (c) when propagated by appropriate means, retains those characters.[***]

Copyrights aside, cultivars are not naturally occurring plants, even if they are allowed to share the same scientific nomenclature as their native forebears. When a plant's binomial scientific name is followed by a capitalized name, possibly set off in quotation marks but not usually italicized, this means the plant is a cultivar, and a cultivar is not a native plant. For example, a *Quercus alba* 'Marcell' is a white oak cultivar cloned by someone who named his creation after a relative. While cultivars do not necessarily pose the same environmental risks

[*]   In botany and zoology, the abbreviation L. indicates that Linneaus was the authority for a species name.
[**]   An environmental group proposed this name in conjunction with the Rainforest Trust in protest against Donald Trump's blindness toward environmental policies.
[***]   The International Code of Nomenclature for Cultivated Plants: Article 2.2.

as non-native plants, they cannot provide the same level of habitat support. To dissimulate a cultivar's shortcomings and to profit from the native plant movement, cultivars are sometimes disguised as "nativars." But by whatever name these mixed breeds are called, they do not support ecosystems as well as native plants and could require more care if they are to thrive.

THE LOW GROUND

"These animals do not know what yesterday and today are but leap about, eat, rest, digest, and leap again; and so from morning to night and from day to day, only briefly concerned with their pleasure and displeasure, enthralled by the moment and for that reason neither melancholy or bored."

—*Man vs. Animal* (1874),
Friedrich Nietzsche

Taking a "nature" tour around a suburban development will illustrate that the best kept turf-grass lawns have almost no pollinators or other insects living there—whether bees, butterflies, or beetles—as turf grass cannot support nearly as many insects as native plants can. And where there are no insects, there are no birds. A staggering 96% of songbirds, even those that subsist on seeds and berries as adults, rely on insects to feed their young. A growing body needs protein, and for birds, the best source of protein is a bug. Birds do not know when a bug is sick with poison and "apocalypse" is the word most scientists use to describe what is happening to the unsuspecting bird population. For wildlife populations are at one in the realm of native plants; they are genetically indisposed to understand the toxic perils of suburbia.

By eliminating turf grass and endowing a suburban property with an infusion of native trees, shrubs, ground covers, and wildflowers, it is certain that the fruits, flowers, and seeds these plants produce will all find ready wildlife takers. Moreover, the decay of the previous season's leaves, twigs, mast, etc., will nourish the insects and fungi that fertilize and enrich the soil. Studies by the US Wildlife Service have shown that even modest increases of native plant cover on suburban properties will raise the number and species of breeding birds, including birds of conservation concern.[*]

Globally, the apocalyptic bells of climate change and ecological collapse have tolled on every continent and threaten all living things. There is little use in asking for whom these bells toll, as all are involved and all have a role to play.

* USDA: Climate Change Resource Center (2013), Olson and Saenz.

CHAPTER 4

Understanding Your Environment

"My grandmother lived in a three-story house that was old even in those days. There was a pear tree in the front yard which was heavily eroded by rain by years of not having any lawn. The picket fence that once enclosed the lawn was gone, too, and people just drove their cars right up to the porch. In the winter the front yard was a mud hole and in the summer it was as hard as a rock. Jack used to curse the front yard as if it were a living thing."
—*Revenge of the Lawn* (1971), Richard Brautigan

THE REVENGE of the Old World upon the New, coming from the toxic effects of a century of cultivating turf grass, is now being visited upon America's suburbanites and its unsuspecting wildlife. A simple remedy to this situation would be to uproot the turf grass, fill the yard with native plants, and let life begin afresh. For, while native and non-native plants can be equally beautiful, non-native plants do not help the environment, nor do they readily cohabit with native plants. Worse, non-native plants often require a toxic mix of chemicals to survive in a foreign land.

There are those who will argue that the evidence of the adverse effect of non-native plants is not conclusive and that exceptions occur. These skeptics further argue that if homeowners and the landscaping industry managed non-native plants appropriately, their impact upon the natural environment would be minimal. However, the risk that their arguments are wrong is great, and thus the Precautionary Principle[*] should be applied, meaning that if a non-native plant cannot, with certainty, be shown to be risk-free, it should not be used to restore a landscape. Certainly, non-natives have their place, in vegetable and flower gardens for the most part, but their present dominance of the suburban landscape puts the entire ecosystem at peril.

HABITAT

Habitat is the entanglement of non-living and living components in a particular environment that is suitable to each living organism's needs. The living components of a terrestrial habitat are members of the plant, animal, and fungal

---

[*] Defined by the United Nations Conference on Environment and Development (June 1992). The Precautionary Principle dictates that where there are threats of serious or irreversible damage to the environment, the absence of full scientific certainty should not be used as a reason for postponing measures to prevent the degradation of the environment.

kingdoms, and their habitat can be defined as the area where all coexist inside a range wherein each can find its own basic requirements. Charles Darwin, in the last paragraph to the later editions of *On the Origin of Species*, described habitat as follows:

It is interesting to contemplate a tangled bank, clothed with many plants of many kinds, with birds singing on the bushes, with various insects flitting about, and with worms crawling through the damp earth, and to reflect that these elaborately constructed forms, so different from each other, and dependent upon each other in so complex a manner, have all been produced by laws acting around us.

Homeowners, before uprooting the grass and planting native species, should consider the characteristics of the wildlife and fungi that could inhabit their habitat.

"Eastern gray squirrel"

ANIMAL KINGDOM BASICS

The Animal Kingdom, as concerns suburban yards, is composed of the following wildlife: (a) mammals, (b) birds, (c) amphibians and reptiles, and (d) insects and worms. The most important non-living component for wildlife is surface water, whether for drinking, bathing, or maintaining moisture. Wildlife habitats differ, because food preferences vary depending on the wildlife species: herbivores eat plants, carnivores need protein, and omnivores want both. The term *wildlife* has come to include all mobile organisms that live wild in an area without being introduced by humans. Terrestrial wildlife can be found in all ecosystems: forests, deserts, plains, and cities and their adjacent suburbs. According to a report issued by the World Wide Fund for Nature (WWF), the global wildlife population has decreased by 52% between 1974 and 2014. While exactly which kinds of wildlife have diminished by 52% is unclear, the WWF's guiding principle is crystal clear: "To stop the degradation of the earth's natural environment and to build a future in which humans live in harmony with nature." Alas, the WWF is focused on fundraising, and their energies are concentrated on regions more politically expedient than suburbia, particularly those that harbor charismatic megafauna such as tigers, whales, panda bears, etc. This is a pity, given that the 174 million Americans who live in the suburbs have a great potential to care for equally valuable, if less charismatic, wildlife. Moreover, American suburbanites have the ways and means to use their own property to improve the environment. While a single sylvan landscape will not trigger a Mount Araratian experience, where an ark docks and lucky pairs of animals file down the walkway, its beauty and usefulness could provide the impetus for the neighbors to join in.

As animals in a shrinking environment struggle for food and water, their paths will cross more often with suburbanites, the more humane of which will hopefully be more inclined to sharing their environment rather than eliminating the wildlife. A threat to the conservation of biodiversity in suburbia is an absence of empathy and understanding of wildlife amongst the suburbanites themselves. *Extinction of experience* is a term used to describe the substantial decline in the amount of time that people spend outdoors and the loss of those diverse experiences that such time in nature entails.[*] Individuals who have had more outdoor experiences are far more likely to have pro-environmental attitudes, and this particularly applies to children. As families spend more time indoors and have less access to natural areas, their familiarity with and perspectives toward wildlife decline. These perceptions of nature set the template for the future willingness of people to invest in the conservation of nature. Given that many more people live in suburbanized landscapes than in previous generations, and that a sylvan landscape can bring back some of the richness and diversity of nature into the suburbs, I hope that such landscaping will motivate future generations to cherish and protect their fellow wildlife.

While there is little that homeowners can do to offset the effects of climate change within a broad landscape, they can affect conditions on their own property that will help wildlife survive a drought. The means of helping wildlife in their time of need can be found in a sylvan landscape, where drought-resistant native plants provide food and host insects and where the refilled birdbath provides a constant source of water. Consideration of the local wildlife and the types of native plants that support this wildlife are the keys to having a yard with a useful habitat.

A. Mammals

Mammals, from the Latin *mamma* (breast), are vertebrate animals characterized by the presence of mammary glands in females, a neocortex (a region of the brain), fur or hair, and three middle ear bones. While mammals such

"Red Fox"

as squirrels, chipmunks, bats, and similar sized critters will be regularly attracted to a sylvan landscape when the trees and shrubs begin to provide shelter and food, it is unlikely they will take up a more permanent residence until the trees have matured. There is also the possibility that a larger mammal may wander in, such as a raccoon, coyote, deer, or bear, but they will also wander out. The trick is to enjoy the larger fauna when the chance arises.

B. Birds

Birds, also known as Aves (from the Latin "avis") or avian dinosaurs (in deference to their ances-

"Baltimore Oriole"

---

[*] "The Extinction of Experience" (2016), Masashi Soga and Kevin Gaston.

tors), are a group of vertebrates characterized by feathers, toothless beaked jaws, the laying of hard-shelled eggs, and four-chambered hearts. When Fraser Darling, a famed British ornithologist, observed "We need time, time, time, to study these delightful little creatures," his field of predilection was the Scottish Highlands, and his overriding concern was the loss of this natural habitat. Fraser Darling also felt that most birds, when faced by the destruction of their habitat, remain social and try to adapt. Despite a lack of similarity between the Scottish Highlands and the American suburbs, a sylvan landscape in a sea of turf grass can lend itself to such feathered social gatherings. The possibility that such a landscape would attract different species of birds is proportional to the growth of the plants and the shelter and edibles that each plant provides. As the sylvan landscape matures, so will the habitat improve, with the result that birds will take up a more permanent residence; they will come to the suburbs to nest and even mate, much like the human components.

C. Amphibians and Reptiles

Amphibians and reptiles are often collectively referred to as herps, herptiles or, with becoming majesty, herpetofauna. The term comes from the Greek root *herpet*, meaning "creeping." Herpetology is the study of ectothermic (cold blooded) tetrapods (four-limbed animals), which fall into four broad categories: lizards

A Cautionary Tale: The English Starling

Eugene Schieffelin, a wealthy and idle scion of one of Manhattan's oldest and most prominent families, was a contemporary of Frederick Olmsted and a great admirer of the latter's signature creation, Central Park. It was Schieffelin's fantasy to introduce all of the birds mentioned in the plays of William Shakespeare into North America, believing that by this singular act he would improve the lot of his less-literate countrymen. His only success came with the transplantation of the English starling, a species with a gift for mimicry. The starling appears in *Henry IV*, when Hotspur considers ways of employing the bird's vocal talents to drive King Henry mad. In 1890, Schieffelin arranged for the importation of 60 pairs of English starlings, had them released into Central Park, and embarked upon his dream. For the first 10 years, these "founder" starlings stayed close to Manhattan. Given the starling's adaptability and diverse dietary preferences, they had spread, by 1942, to the West Coast, and can now be found as far away as Alaska. Scientists estimate that the descendants of these airborne thespians now number more than 200 million, every one of them adversely impacting the ecosystem and the economy. Today's biologists consider Schieffelin to have been an eccentric at best, a lunatic at worst, and a caution to those who would tamper with nature.*

* *Tinkering with Eden* (2001), Kim Todd.

and salamanders, turtles, frogs and toads, and snakes (which have residual limbs). Generally, reptiles have scales and claws on their feet and are less dependent on moisture than amphibians; amphibians are not scaled, their clawless feet are covered with skin, and they are more likely to migrate to breeding grounds than reptiles. Suburban development has negatively affected the habitat of these environmentally valuable creatures by creating hazardous zones, such as roads, between important habitat features.

"Damselfly"

D. Insects and Worms

Insects and worms* are both classified as animals. Rather than join a long-standing debate over whether or not these species' shared traits merits a more complex and distinctive classification,** it is easier to conclude that both, during some stage of their life careers, have a certain *icky* factor. Curiously, this same icky factor makes both worms and insects extremely appetizing to almost all wildlife, particularly themselves. Should more specifics be needed: worms are invertebrates, with elongated, cylindrical tube-like bodies, without limbs or eyes; and insects make up a very large and difficult to categorize group that tend to have notched bodies and quivering appendages. The most diverse insect types appear to have coevolved with flowering plants.

Insects and worms require space, sometimes a different concept than habitat. Space can range from the local, in the case of ants, to the continental, in the case of the monarch butterfly. Often, a fertile, pesticide-free yard is all the space the more static of ground-delving worms or insects require. But regardless of the ultimate size of the space, it must have a functional connectivity for foraging, mating, and resting.*** A sylvan landscape has the possibility of extending the connectivity and contributing to the quality of such spaces. For example, wildflowers are often an essential component of space, and planting regionally specific wildflowers, often in what is referred to as a pollinator garden, adds to that space, as insect pollinators move pollen from the male to the female part of the flower, whether on the same or different plants, ensuring the survival of both the insect and the flora, as well as the quality of the space. Charles Darwin, was a keen observer of the bumblebees' specialized use of space: "I have found that the visits of bees, if not indispensable, are at least beneficial to the fertilization of our clovers; but humble-bees alone visit the red clover, as the other bees cannot reach the nectar." Native bees, North America's most important pollinators, are dependent on just such space.

---

* The word *worm* comes from the term *Verme*, an obsolete grouping used by Linneaus.
** The debate started in 1793 when the French invertebrate specialist Jean-Baptiste Lamarck called the *Verme*s a species of chaos and split the Linnaen category into four new categories.
*** "Solutions for humanity on how to conserve insects," Biological Conservation 242 (2020).

A Cautionary Tale: The Honeybee

The First Coming of the honeybee (*Apis mellifera*) to North America, as related in *The Book of Mormon,* was roughly 3,700 years before Columbus was credited with the discovery of the same continent.* These pagan honeybees were ferried to America by a disgruntled tribe of Judaic Mesopotamians, followers of the prophet Jared, who fled Babylon sometime after the construction of the Tower of Babel and shortly before it was wrathfully overturned. As related in Ether: "And they did also carry with them deseret, which by interpretation, is the honeybee; and thus they did carry swarms of bees."** It was Joseph Smith Jr., a prophet and founder of Mormonism, who translated the language of the Jaredites and revealed that the term "deseret," in the extinct Jaredish tongue, meant "honeybee." After the Jaredites and their honeybees left Babylon, around 2200 BCE, they wandered, perhaps east, perhaps west, but certainly far from the land of Nod until they reached an ocean where divinely constructed and supernaturally lighted barges awaited to carry them to the New World. While the histories and travels of the Jaredites and their honeybees are fascinating, neither of these invasive species survived in the New World long after 441 BCE, albeit the written records of each are far more complete than the archeological records of either.

The Second Coming of the honeybee to North America was again made by boat, this time aboard the good ship *Discovery,* bound to the New World from London. In March 1622 BCE, the *Discovery* landed in Jamestown, Virginia, carrying vital cargo that included "Pidgeons, Peacockes, Maistues, and Beehives." Once landed, these resourceful insects promptly managed to escape domestication, forming swarms and setting up housekeeping in hollow trees or other cavities just as they had been doing in their native lands. By 1776, they had swarmed their way to Michigan. In 1848, the honeybee came to Utah, this time by hives carried on the backs of Mormon wagons fleeing from Nauvoo. In the wagon trains of their persecuted keepers, these honeybees traveled west, crossed the Mississippi River, and finally swarmed in what failed to become the State of Honeybee.

In 1850, the State of Honeybee came close to realization when the Mormons, after having successfully endured the trials and tribulations that accompany the establishment of new religions, petitioned the federal government for statehood as the State of Deseret. To sweeten their petition, the Mormon fathers gifted the Washington Monument with a foundational Deseret stone, replete with carved beehive and bees. The stone was accepted and eventually mortared into the Washington Monument at the 220-foot level. The pious generosity of the Church of the Latter Day Saints notwithstanding, Congress rejected their bid for a theocracy and named the region the Utah Territory in the mistaken belief that its native tribes called themselves Utes.

Despite the honeybees' successes, setbacks, and invasive character, the *Apis melli*

---

*   *Book of Mormon*, Ether 1–15.
** *Book of Mormon*, Ether 2:3.

fera is now Utah's state insect. Today's honeybees are raised and managed like farm animals, and there is no longer any risk that they will suffer the fate of their Jaredite forebears. As many foods grown on modern farmlands are non-native and inhospitable to wild pollinators, agriculture has become dependent upon vast numbers of commercially managed honeybees to pollinate crops. But the honeybee does not always live in harmony with America's nature, competing with native bees for food, spreading disease amongst their brethren, and upsetting the balance of plant species, all of which is leaving many species of native bees with a diminishing habitat and ultimate extinction.

"Honeybee"

The Effects of Climate Change on Wildlife

Whether or not climate change constitutes a trial or a retribution for the inconstant human species, it falls hardest upon the blameless wildlife. During the South's long hot summer of 2019, almost no rain fell and the highs often spurred heat indexes over 100°. When it is extremely hot and dry, plants bear less fruit, berries, seeds, and even their leaves, stems, and branches become less palatable. In drought years, female mammals produce less milk and raise fewer young. Because 96% of terrestrial birds eat insects, and insect populations plummet during a drought, nesting adults are struggling to feed their young. Wildflowers have withered and died, leaving pollinators without nectar or pollen. Migrating birds that passed over the South during the drought have found less food, compromising their ability to complete the flight to their wintering grounds.

"Chanterelle"

FUNGAL KINGDOM BASICS

Fungi occupy their own biological kingdom and are absolutely essential to the health of all ecosystems. Fungi form literal connections between organisms and, like Darwin's "tangled bank," remind humans that all life forms, including ourselves, are connected.

The vast majority of the fungal biomass consists of an underground trove of interwoven threadlike hyphae growing in plant tissues and in the soil. Less than 5% of the estimated 1.5 million species of fungi have been described, and their exact roles and interactions in ecosystems are largely unknown. We do know that fungi play a critical role in the fertilization of the soil by enhancing decomposition and recycling nutrients. Additionally, fungi can have symbiotic relationships with plants and biological control over other fungi. Those fungi that can be readily seen, and are better known as mushrooms, are distinguished from other fungi by their aboveground fruiting structures. Annual variation in the timing and emergence of mushrooms is largely influenced by temperature and precipitation. Fungi fall into two broad categories: those that feed upon decaying woody plants, the saprotrophic; and those that have a symbiotic relationship with the plant's roots, the mycorrhizae.

- Saprotrophic fungi play a quasi-religious role in ensuring that living things return to the dust from which they sprang. The process of plant growth, decline, and decay followed by the reabsorption of the released compounds is generally referred to as nutrient cycling. But regardless of how a woody plant or its parts die or decompose, only saprotrophic fungi can accomplish the final step of breaking down the hardening

A SERAL COMMUNITY IN SUBURBIA

A suburban community, by definition, lies between the urban and the rural, the former harboring but a few of a region's wildlife species, the latter harboring most all. As previously explained, a disruption in a climax community can provide the opening needed to entertain a seral community wherein smaller wildlife can find food, shelter, and nesting sites. Such openings also provide "edge," a transition zone wherein different natural communities or successional plant stages come together. A sylvan landscape in a suburban community is a similar disruption in the vast swathe of turf grass that can also provide edge, not unlike an opening in a forest. Admittedly, openings in a forest occur as a result of larger disturbances—"whether insects, fires, or floods"—whereas a sylvan landscape is a disturbance that can be achieved without inviting the remaining plagues of Egypt into suburbia—"whether boils, frogs, or blood"—and one that will also fulfill needs of the local wildlife.

As demonstrated, an understanding of a region's pre-Columbian evolution, the impact of early European settlement on the region's environment, and the environmental ravages of the past two centuries are the prerequisites for making an optimal choice of regional native plants. However, the extent to which the sylvan landscape reflects the vegetative components of nearby habitats will determine which wildlife could actually arrive. In choosing the mix of native plants for the new landscape, there are also seasonal factors to consider. Because during the course of a year, predictable changes occur in the availability of food sources for wildlife, designing the landscape with seasonal availability of food in mind improves the chance of attracting wildlife year-round. Spring flowers, summer berries, and fall fruits are obvious choices; wildlife will seek new food sources because some are depleted due to the natural cycles of production. There are also yearly shortages of particular foods, particularly in the late fall and winter, to be attentive to. Mast, for example, is the dry fruit from woody plants and includes samara from maple, elm and ash, pine seeds, and nuts from oak, hickory, beech, witch-hazel, and black walnut. Given that mast is the primary fall and winter food for most wildlife species, a combination of mast-producing trees and shrubs is useful in the event that one type fails to produce for one or more years. Fruits and seeds are also widely sought when insect populations become dormant in fall or winter, and the seeds that remain on the plant during the winter months are lifesavers for many. The structure, density, and height of vegetation will also contribute to wildlife's use of the property's new landscape; it provides them with different levels of cover and extra opportunities for foraging. A sylvan landscape should be designed so that as it matures it will have both vertical and horizontal structural diversity. Vertically, the ground-level plants, the shrub-rows, the smaller trees, and the upper canopy trees—four levels in all—form the vertical foundation. Horizontally, plant communities should flow and blend into one other, facilitating wildlife circulation.

PART II

Transforming Your Lawn

CHAPTER 5

Basics of Landscape Design

When the proofs, the figures, were ranged in columns before me,
When I was shown the charts and diagrams, to add, divide, and measure them,
When I sitting heard the astronomer where he lectured
with much applause in the lecture-room,
How soon unaccountable I became tired and sick,
Till rising and gliding out I wander'd off by myself,
In the mystical moist night-air, and from time to time,
Look'd up in perfect silence at the stars.
—"When I Heard the Learn'd Astronomer" (1865), Walt Whitman

BECAUSE THE COMPENDIUM of laws, rules, and principles of landscape design—"the charts and diagrams to add, divide, and measure from"—can weigh a person down, I have brushed these tenets aside. Nor do I recommend their study to homeowners. Rather, per the chapter's precedent, I have advised homeowners to gird themselves with the armaments of the ecological warrior by studying their region's ecological history and socioeconomic evolution; examining the forests adjacent to their community; learning which plants are native to their region; and deciding which native plants would best support the local environment.

Yet there are a few earthly items that need to be considered before "wandering into the mystical moist night-air" of sylvan landscaping: (1) which kind of soil underlies the homeowner's property; (2) which types of hardscape would best serve the homeowner's needs; and (3) which techniques and tools are required to map out the property.

1. SOIL

Soil analysis is a process that determines the inorganic and organic composition of the soil: the former being the soil type and the latter indicating the levels of nutrients, acidity, contaminants, etc. The results of this analysis will indicate the soil's chemical, physical, and biological potential to ensure a plant's nutrition and growth.

Soil Types

The three basic types of soil are sand, silt, and clay, but most soil is composed of a mixture of each and called loam. How these types are mixed will determine the soil's texture, meaning how it feels, looks, and drains.

SAND is composed of small pieces of weathered rock that are fairly coarse and loose. Water is easily able to drain through sand, and while this is good for drainage, it is not good for growing plants because sandy soil will not hold the necessary water or nutrients.

SILT can be thought of as fine sand that will hold water much better than coarse sand. If you hold a handful of dry silt, it will feel almost like flour. If you add water to this handful of silt, it will do a fair job of holding the water and will feel slick and smooth.

CLAY is very fine-grained soil that does not accommodate many plant species. Its particles are even smaller than silt, so there is very little space between the fine grains for air or water to circulate. Clay does not drain well or provide space for plants to flourish. If you add water to clay it can be molded into pottery or bricks.

LOAM can be considered a fourth type of soil, even though it is a combination of sand, silt, and clay. The composition of loam for plants will vary depending on how much of each soil type is present. For healthy plants, an evenly mixed loam is a preferred type of soil because it holds moisture, supports nutrients, and allows for good drainage.

Soil Fertility

Soil is said to be the womb within which fertility develops. In healthy soil will be found the tiniest members of the plant and animal kingdoms, collectively referred to as microbes or microorganisms, whose role is to digest and decompose organic matter, a process that renders the soil fertile. A soil with the highest number of microbes is considered to be the most fertile, and the microbes' continued felicity ensures the permanent existence of nutrients. Native plants growing in such soils require neither fertilizers nor pesticides to thrive. Soil acidity is a more complex question. There are three major reasons why a soil can become too acidic: rainfall and leaching, acidic parent material, and the decay of certain organic matter. While there are many ways of adjusting a soil's acidity, the use of natural compost will help keep the right balance.

Given that the soil underlying the turf grass of almost every suburban property has most likely been denatured, it is advisable, before considering a sylvan landscape, to have a clear understanding of the results of the soil analysis. For if native plants are to be transplanted into soil where turf grass once grew, it pays to be wary of the pesticide-laden underbelly of Satan's own lawn because damnation may well await an unwary native plant. In such Dantesque scenarios, the toxicity of the soil under a manicured front lawn can be likened to the seventh circle of hell, whereas the soil in the more temperate backyard usually harbors only lesser imps and demons. If the analysis shows that the soil in the front yard is indeed damned, it should be replaced. As for the backyard soil, some sort of mild exorcism, such as by overplanting or rototilling, could suffice.

2. HARDSCAPE

Hardscape consists of the nonliving items that could be built, purchased, and/or installed on the landscape.

Primary Paths

Because suburban homes tend to have an entry walkway and a driveway, these items will be collectively referred to as primary paths. If such paths are made of concrete or any other impermeable material, they could be replaced with a permeable material that will allow water to seep through and return to the soil. Such replacements can be high-ticket items. However, if the existing primary paths are in poor condition, this may be the moment to consider an improved design, using more eco-friendly material.

Secondary Paths

Suburban properties usually have secondary paths by design or accident. Secondary paths keep people's feet dry and provide safe passage from the house to the more useful parts of the yard. In a natural setting, a well-designed secondary path can also shape and define the landscape by visually and physically connecting its different segments to create a more aesthetic and functional whole. Given that a secondary path does not get as much foot traffic as a primary path, it can be made narrower and less obtrusive and can be covered with mulch rather than with harder or more costly materials.

Mulch

Mulch is a layer of organic or inorganic material that is laid upon the surface of the soil. Reasons for covering secondary paths with organic mulch include the conservation of soil moisture, improved fertility, and reduced weed growth. As a mulching of a path in a landscape should contribute to the health of the plants, special

attention should be given to the use of native organic mulch. With the base needs of turf grass no longer an issue, organic mulch paths can be safely nestled near trees, shrubs, and ground covers. Nor will such mulch paths need hard borders; spillage will enrich and insulate the soil near the plants. Native organic wood chips are an excellent choice for mulch and often contain wild mushroom spores. Wetting by rain and dew affects the longevity and usefulness of any organic mulch, and so it will need to be rejuvenated every 2 to 5 years.

During the first years after planting, generous mulching around trees or shrubs will keep precious water in the soil, deter the growth of weeds, and reduce erosion. For trees, regardless of the species, a mulch cover of 5 feet in diameter is advised for the first few years. If the mulch encirclement is found attractive, it can be rejuvenated. Or, after 2 to 3 years, the native ground cover can be allowed to encroach upon the mulch, eventually encircle the trunk of the tree, and perform much the same function. Shrubs will require less of a mulched bed and the mulch can be overlaid with raked-up leaves in the following year.

Paved Space

The usefulness of a paved space in the backyard is proportional to the degree to which it can enhance the lives or satisfy the whims of the homeowners. A strategically designed paved space, one that will be solid to the foot, permeable, and of reasonable dimensions, offers the surest possibility of placing the residents within the ambit of the new landscape. Whether designed for rest, dining, or socializing, the paved space should be accessible via a secondary path. If drainage or available space is a constraint, a raised wooden deck is a viable option. The paved space should also be supportive of

the chair, table, and bench, while providing desirable measures of sun and shade.

Accessories

A bench, placed in an appropriate spot in the yard, can be a perch from which to appreciate the budding habitat. Such a bench sits in opposition to the front-porch rocking chair, wherein the rockers wave endlessly to the passersby, or the backyard hammock, from where the supine contemplate the heavens. Benches are best when they are of solid construction and modest beauty. A birdhouse is often more ornamental than a useful nest, whereas a birdbath is a must; it will attract different species of birds that will drink, bathe, and cool off in it. If a birdbath is placed 3 feet off the ground and in a partially open space, birds will have a better chance to see and avoid predators. A water depth of 2 inches is right for most species. The bird-bath should be regularly refilled and cleaned in order to provide a reliable source of clean water, a vital component for any ecosystem. As for the style of the birdbath, Oscar Wilde's advice remains appropriate: "One must live up to one's doorknobs." Fences, trellises, and pergolas are useful elements for privacy and for plants to climb on.

Compost Area

The compost area can be simple. A shallow hole dug in a corner of the backyard can transform a natural landscape's fallings and clippings into fertilizer at a leisurely pace. For the average suburban property, an 8-foot-by-4-foot pit dug to a depth of 18 inches should be adequate. The dirt dug out of the pit can be placed behind the pit's sides and back and graded back down to ground level. There are more elaborate composting systems that are used to produce rich compost

for vegetable and flower gardens, but they often involve kitchen waste and chemicals, both to be avoided. The idea is merely to return the nutrients to the soil. Depending on the climate, the first year's detritus will compact over the course of the second winter and leave space for the following year's clippings and fallings. In the next spring, mix the compost up with a sturdy rake or shovel and spread it around the shrub's roots. Repeat the process annually. Such compost will be drier, coarser, and the perfect fertilizer for native plants. The dirt stacked behind and on the sides of the pit is an ideal place for a small, easily fertilized pollinator garden.

3. TECHNIQUE

At this point, the property surrounding the home should seem like a blank canvas, waiting for a sylvan landscape design that, if executed, will align the property with nature, the aesthetics of the homeowner, and the mores of the community. If so, it is now time to prepare the blank canvas by drawing up a site map that will show the outside dimensions of the house, the perimeter lines of the property, and any other important features. For a head start on the house and perimeter dimensions, use the plot plan that should have come with the property's deed of purchase. If this plan cannot be found, perhaps the mortgage company or town hall has a copy. However, the physical acts of measuring the property and drawing up a site plan will provide the best insights into the property's potential. Also, the new measurements may nip a boundary dispute in the bud.

During the first walkabout,* take note of the cardinal point of the compass upon which the house faces, meaning north, east, south, etc. Then take note of the topography of both the

---

* A walkabout is a rite of passage in Australian aboriginal society that requires a fledgling male member of the tribe to wander in the wilderness in preparation for a spiritual makeover.

front and backyard, paying special attention to which locations are sloped and the slopes' effect on drainage (there may be soggy areas). Take note of any neighboring trees that may border your own property.

Given that drawing up a site map for one's own property may well be a one-time-only affair, it is advisable to design by hand rather than to purchase landscaping software, which takes time and practice to master. Moreover, the skills required to design by hand are well within a homeowner's reach and can result in a better comprehension of the job at hand and an above average appreciation of the final landscape.

The tools required to map out a landscape of a suburban property are as follows: your phone's camera, a 100-foot tape measure, small stakes, a pad of graph paper, ruler, colored pencils, a circle template, a French curve set, a drafting compass, and a pad of tracing paper with similar dimensions as the graph paper. There is probably also a feature on your phone that will indicate the points of the compass.

Photograph the Property

Begin embarking on the creation of a site map, obtaining a neutral vision of what a property looks like from all angles by taking pictures of the property from three viewpoints: the outside looking in, the inside looking out, and mid-backyard looking around in a circle. Begin by walking clockwise around the property perimeters and taking a picture from each successive angle, perhaps a dozen in all. Label these pictures in the order taken, such as Out-1, Out-2, or Out-3, for this is how the neighbors see the property. Then, moving clockwise around the inside of the house, take pictures looking out from the windows and doors. Label the pictures in the order taken, such as In-1, In-2, or In-3, for

this is how you see the property from the inside of the house. Finally, standing in the center of the backyard, take another set of pictures while turning clockwise. Label these pictures in the order taken, such as Back-1, Back-2, or Back-3, for this is how users of the paved space will see the property. Reviewing these pictures on a casual basis will be of great help when it comes to developing ideas for your design.

Draw a Site Plan

Using the 100-foot tape, measure the perimeter of the property. If a side is longer than the tape, mark the 100-foot spot with a stake and continue from there. Once the perimeter's dimensions are known, choose a scale that will allow the property to be drawn on a single sheet of graph paper. Once the outline of the property has been drawn, annotate its dimensions and calculate the total square footage. If the property contains strange curves and angles, make an educated guess at the total square footage.[*] The next step will be to locate the house, primary paths, and any other hardscape within the property. Starting from the lower left corner of the property, measure the perpendicular distances from a corner of the house to the two nearest edges of the property. Continuing clockwise, measure the dimension of each side to each corner of the house, including decks, attached terraces, and primary paths. Indicate all the dimensions on the site plan. Calculate the total square footage of the house and hardscape. Using the same measuring techniques, locate the tree trunks and shrubs. Estimate the canopy size of the trees and indicate such by a circle. Measure and include the shrubbery. Once the size and location of the property, the primary paths, and the plants have been determined, call this Site Plan A. Make multiple cop-

---

[*]   Hint: Count the little squares and fractions thereof.

ies of Site Plan A as templates for designing your new landscape.

With a copy of Site Plan A in hand, take a walk around the property and annotate the plan to show where the grass flourishes and where it does not, as well as soggy areas. If the property is not level, does the relief offer the possibility of better drainage? Pay attention to and indicate changes in slope; plants requiring dry and well-drained soil will fare better near the peak of the slope, whereas water-hungry plants will fare better near the base. Note the compass points, too, which regulate from which direction the sun shines and the wind blows. An example of a site plan follows:

Any attempt to design in nature's mold is but an experiment, but, as with any experiment, study, patience, and observation are the best methods of improving the experiment's chances of success. Designing a sylvan landscape is just such an experiment, but if the design is well thought out and carefully executed, there is a high probability that, should the design be executed, the property will be brought back into line with nature. For these reasons, the homeowner has been counseled to:

STUDY YOUR ECOSYSTEM: Examine the history of your region's ecosystems to discover how these systems have been modified or damaged, and for what reasons.

KNOW THE REGION'S NATIVE PLANTS: Study the plants that are native to your region and choose some favorites, plus some that would be the most useful to the local environment.

TAKE STOCK OF YOUR PROPERTY: Test your property's soil, examining the property's drainage and sun exposure. Determine its better angles. Measure the property and draw up a site plan.

The next step is to decide upon a strategy that will best exploit all the potential of the property to care for the household's needs and to benefit the local environment.

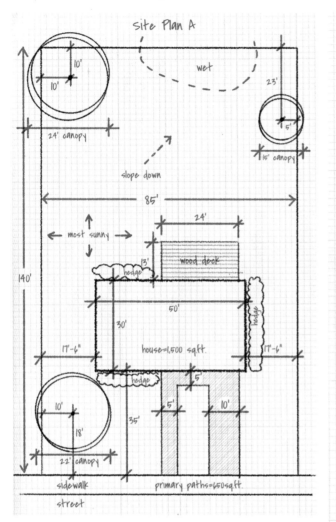

Site Plan A

wet

slope down

24' canopy

10'

10'

23'

5'

15' canopy

85'

24'

most sunny

wood deck

13'

hedge

140'

50'

30'

hedge

house=1,500 sqft.

17'-6"

17'-6"

hedge

10'

18'

22' canopy

35'

5'

5'

5'

10'

sidewalk

street

primary paths=650sqft.

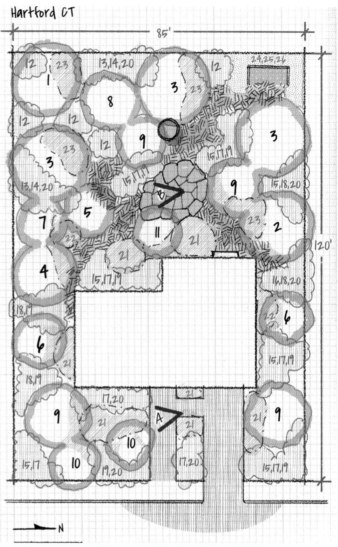

Hartford CT

85'

120'

N

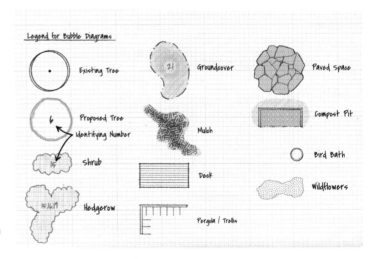

Legend for Bubble Diagrams

Existing Tree

Proposed Tree

Identifying Number

Shrub

Hedgerow

Groundcover

Mulch

Deck

Pergola / Trellis

Paved Space

Compost Pit

Bird Bath

Wildflowers

Sample blueprints including an existing site plan (top left), landscape design plans (top right), and a legend (bottom right).

CHAPTER 6

Basics of Sylvan Design

"The waving line is the 'line of beauty' and the serpentine line
is the 'line of grace.' These two lines are the lines most varied in
form, and they contribute most to producing beauty."
—*The Analysis of Beauty* (1753), William Hogarth

IT HAS BEEN long held and convincingly argued that curves are more beautiful than straight lines, an opinion embraced by the author and the inspiration for the arrangement of plants in a sylvan landscape. Straight rows of conical poplars bespeak Italian landscaping, neatly trimmed linear hedges denote the English style, and symmetry defines the French outlook. The beauty of a sylvan landscape design is based upon the asymmetrical groupings of trees and shrubs curving around and away from the hard right angles and straight lines of architecture. A straight line is the shortest distance between two points, a curved line takes a longer path, and a wavy line takes the longest route. It follows that wavy lines of trees and shrubs in a sylvan landscape will provide the greatest opportunities for a variety of edge conditions.

The curves of trees arise from the nature of their crowns, for trees are fractal in nature. Benoit Mandelbrot,[*] a polymath with broad interests in science and nature, defined fractals as continuous patterns that are self-similar across different scales. He found new meaning in irregular curves, opining that "Clouds are not spheres, mountains are not cones, coastlines are not circles . . . ." A tree is self-similar,

in that a small piece of the tree looks somewhat like the entire tree. The natural curves of a tree are formed by the repetition of a simple process over and over: it sprouts out of the ground, splits into branches, each of these branches split into new branches, and so on. At each point in the process, it is as if two new, smaller trees emerge, and the new branches can be thought of as the next generation of new trees.

The curves of shrubs only exist as latent characteristics and must be brought to the fore by trimming and pruning. The Latin word *toparius* refers to a gardener who creates ornamental landscapes, and topiary is the horticultural practice of training perennial plants to develop and maintain clearly defined shapes, geometric or fanciful. Once planted in arced rows, pruning and trimming shrubs can further refine their curves.

If set in a harmonious fashion—an attribute of landscaping—the combined curves of the trees and shrubs can make the property resemble a verdant oasis to the neighbors and a forest glade to the homeowner, thus resolving the social dissonance that may follow in the wake of abandoning the turf-grass standard. But from where did the concept of landscaping in harmonious fashion arise? It came from gardening. In antiq-

---

[*]   *The Fractal Geometry of Nature* (1982), Benoit Mandelbrot.

uity, all the great civilizations set down rules for designing gardens. Later civilizations absorbed and modified these rules in ways particular to themselves, their habitats, and their purses. It wasn't until the late 18th century that theories of landscaping emerged as an outgrowth of garden design for the likes of manor houses, palaces, and religious complexes, when outdoor areas, parks, and landmarks were landscaped to achieve social–behavioral or aesthetic outcomes.

Given that the American suburbs were not developed until World War II, there was no theory for suburban landscape design, only the procedure followed by developers: step one, place the house prominent and center on the landscape; step two, ring the house with the landscape; and step three, repeat in regular geometric intervals. A turf-grass yard with a trimmed hedge under the house's front windows is the typical result. Accordingly, a toxically boring landscape is the most pervasive feature of suburbia.

The basic premise of sylvan landscaping, that of the juxtaposition of the visions of oasis and glade, can be achieved by positioning the trees and shrubs so that they curve in relation to each other, rather than being used to border the house or other geometric forms on the property. The house, the traditional focus of suburban landscape design, now becomes a foil for the sylvan landscape which, beautiful unto itself, will neither slight the house nor offend the neighbors. However, the beauty of a sylvan landscape depends on more than a careful arrangement of plants. There are three properties of crucial consequence to be taken into consideration: variety, fitness, and ecology.

VARIETY: How great a share variety plays in producing beauty may be seen in the variety of the shapes and colors of the plants themselves. Variety seems of little use other than that of entertaining the eye. That all senses delight in variety and are averse to sameness is a valuable notion that can be applied to landscape design. Rather than just using one or two species of trees and shrubs and a single ground cover, the design should show an abundance of all, given they are both native and compatible.

FITNESS: The fitness of the plants to the landscape, for which every individual plant is chosen and then shaped by nature or art, has perhaps the greatest consequence to the design as a whole in that a sylvan landscape demands that turf grass be replaced by native plants. Given that turf grass currently blankets an average of 60% of a suburban property, new and exciting plant dynamics will emerge. Before assembling these new plant communities into the design, the homeowner must first consider the fitness of each tree or shrub to cohabit with the other, with root systems, crown sizes, and growth rates all taken into consideration.

ECOLOGY: As welcome as a full-scale infusion of native plants sans herbicides and pesticides might be, it takes careful thought to conjure up the right plant mix to entice some of the departed wildlife to return. The choice of plants, relative to the food and/or shelter each provides, must excite the expectations of those critters that may still be able to burrow, crawl, walk, creep, leap, or fly back into the neighborhood. While creatures of a less amusing nature could also venture back, be they raccoons, coyotes, or bears, the equanimity of an ecologist's heart would not be strained.

While the tenets of native plant and anti-lawn movements can meet many of the above criteria, particularly that of improving the environment, they contribute but little to the art of landscaping; good morals do not guarantee good landscapes. To achieve a sylvan design—mantra: oasis and glade—other factors come into play: overall plant strategies; a separate strategy per plant species; and the technique required to put the design on paper.

1. PLANT STRATEGIES

Plant Succession

Not every native plant readily cohabitates with the other: some thrive in dry soil, others in wet, and a sylvan landscape must have the capacity to support its own ecosystem. Your design scheme must take into account the hierarchy of plant succession, which is a non-seasonal cumulative change in the type of plant species that occupies a given area through time. Plant succession involves the cycle of colonization, establishment, and extinction, all of which act on the participating plant species. To illustrate what occurs in a natural setting:

- When a forest fire burns off the vegetation and the dust and ash settle, wildflowers and grasses will fill the cleared space, followed by shrubs and tree seedlings. As tree seedlings take root and grow, the shrubs and grasses will diminish. Ultimately the taller trees will dominate the landscape, whereas only shade-tolerant shrubs and grasses remain to cover the forest floor.
- When an aged tree dies and falls, there is an increase of light reaching the forest floor that results in an increase of light-tolerant plants and a decrease of the less tolerant. Smaller trees grow rapidly when released from the shade and may form bushy circles at the base of the fallen tree. It often hap-

pens that a single tree will come to dominate, take the place of the fallen tree, and the process begins anew.

- A plant succession cycle can easily take centuries. Understanding it is essential to choosing and positioning the plants in your sylvan vision. Here, unlike naturally occurring scenarios, where openings are randomly repopulated by neighboring plant communities that then strive for an equilibrium, the homeowner is curating the types of plants, their age, and their placement, thereby eliminating inter-plant competition. The trees and shrubs will not be planted from seed but rather as thriving plants set in appropriate juxtaposition to the other. The ground cover will be similarly positioned to profit from the extra sunlight during the time it takes for the trees and shrubs to grow and start casting their shade.

Plant Growth

Another key element to landscape design is to be able to envision what the new landscape will look like at future intervals. Mature sizes and forms of trees and shrubs are influenced by natural variations in the soil and climate as well as human influences. The visual aspect of plants will also change with the seasons. Mature trees have the most powerful visual impact, but while they are growing in, shrubbery will be the landscape's prominent feature. There are also many pruning possibilities for trees and shrubs that shape their future forms. Visualize these volumes within the photographs you've taken long before the physical onset of the landscaping, considering as many of these variables' interactions over time as changing volumes, changing color. This will improve your layout; it will be possible to imagine what the landscape will look like after 2, 5, and 10 years. To begin, imag-

ine that, at the time of planting, the trees were 4 to 6 feet tall, the shrubs were a year old, and the ground cover came from seedlings or seeds:

- By the fall of the 2nd year, the trees should be 2 to 6 feet higher, depending on their growth rate, and, in some instances, no longer in need of irrigation or support. The shrubs will have profited from the full sunlight and become substantial. The ground cover should look complete.
- By the fall of the 5th year, the trees will have more branches and leaves and will be adding color and texture to the landscape as well as casting some shade. The shrubs will have been trimmed to their desired shapes. The ground cover will be fully established, although the trees may have altered the sun and shade patterns, and one type of ground cover may have encroached upon the space destined for another. The landscape will start to have a finished appearance.
- By the spring of the 10th year, many of the tree's crowns will have filled out, the yard will have its shady spots, and the shrubs and ground cover will have adjusted to different measures of sun and shade.

Given that the choice of each plant for the sylvan landscape will require a balance of aesthetic and ecological visions, it is best to proceed slowly and carefully with the selection of each. Keep in mind that the landscape is certain to look raw just after planting, no matter which varieties of plants have been selected, but after a few years' growth the landscape will round out and soften. By the fifth year, it should be attractive, and by the tenth year, the landscape might look as if it had always been there. A home nestled in an oasis by a glade.

It is true that after 10 years, the vicissitudes of nature and the vagaries of gardening may

have modified the landscape beyond what the homeowner intended. The landscape may be more beautiful than imagined.

Effects of Light and Shade

While turf grass and vegetables require 6 to 8 hours of direct sunlight to prosper, a naturally occurring forest glade does not. In a sylvan landscape, shade, the bane of sod, now helps keep moisture in the soil and the house cool in summer. In winter, the shade will disappear with the leaves and the added sunlight will help keep the house warm. The increased number of trees will have a kaleidoscopic effect on the influence of light and upon the landscape. Consider, for example, the effect of morning light, when the sun is in the east. Toward the west,

every tree will be seen in full light without shadow; if one turns north or south, the trees will be seen in both the light and the shade; and if one looks east, toward the coming of the sun, the trees are backlit silhouettes. These light and shade interactions will slowly tint the atmosphere as day moves toward night.

2. SPECIES STRATEGIES

Trees

If a suburban yard is to harbor its own ecosystem in reasonable time, using only large trees with slow growth rates will neither provide much immediate gratification nor support wildlife. Nor will the property be able to sustain so many large trees when they mature. Including small to medium-sized trees with moderate to fast growth rates builds a more complete ecosystem that will coalesce at a faster rate. Comfort can be taken from the fact that almost all trees have the capacity to live for at least a hundred years.

As shade, the eternal enemy of turf grass, loses its sting, the number of trees that can be planted in residential neighborhoods increases dramatically. Considering their size, visual impact, and ecological importance at maturity, trees are the least expensive of plants. The groupings of trees will become the sylvan landscape's focal points as they mature. The practicality of such arrangements is also to be considered, for example: light-textured deciduous trees with moderate to fast growth rates, placed closer to the house, will neatly parcel out the sun and shade during summer months and not block the sunshine during winter months. Generally, the backyard will offer more latitude for planting trees than a front yard encumbered by primary paths and a sidewalk. If there are healthy, mature, non-native trees in the yard, they should not be removed, but rather incorporated in the overall design.

The total amount of trees that can be contained in a yard does not depend upon the diameters of their mature crowns, which can overlap slightly. Tree crowns can, and often do, extend beyond the property's boundaries, although it is not advised that they overhang the house. Nor is the size of a tree's crown at maturity necessarily proportional to the tree's height, as tall trees can have small crowns and vice versa. There is also the height of the first branches above the ground to consider, as there are small trees with high crowns that can be walked under and large trees with low crowns that must be walked around or climbed into.

If a general design rule is needed, irrespective of a tree's particularities, medium-sized

to large trees are best placed near the borders of the property, small to medium-sized trees should be planted just in front of the larger trees, and very small trees should be placed toward the center. Using smaller trees with larger crowns can favor the landscape's appearance at the 2-, 5-, and 10-year milestones and, if arranged artfully, will further enhance the landscape's appearance when they reach maturity.

Shrubs

While a squared hedge is a form of topiary that satisfies the usual requirements of traditional landscaping, a more natural approach would be arrange the shrubs in maze-like patterns interspersed between the trees. The nature of these shrub-rows, for our purposes, will be taken to mean 2 to 4 shrubs, of different varieties, planted together in a curved or an angled formation, and trimmed to varying heights. Ideally, such a shrub-row would be a mix of deciduous and evergreen shrubs, wherein each contributes to the shape and color of the row as well as bearing different berries, nuts, flowers, etc. For a shrub-row to be successful, the maxim "right plant, right place" must apply to every shrub chosen; each individual shrub must be able to live in harmony with its companion, enjoying the same soil, light, and water conditions. The individual shrubs in a shrub-row should be set 3 to 4 feet apart in the desired curve or angle, the idea being to let them grow used to one another, their outer branches intermingling.

Ground Covers

Nature abhors a vacuum. Any yard space not filled by tree trunks, shrubs, or hardscape must be occupied by ground cover lest noxious weeds creep in. Nor should the new landscape design forego any of the aesthetic benefits of ground cover, as it will reflect the curves created by the shrubbery while adding its own color, shape, and texture to the mix. There are evergreen ground covers that thrive in the shade and that can be used to encircle the bases of trees. Other types of ground cover, deciduous or evergreen, can surround and enhance the shrubbery. Moss, where it will grow, is beautiful.

For the tranquility of the community, it is best to avoid any front yard ground cover that looks like it needs mowing, for it will be in the front yard that the hammer of the maintenance codes falls hardest. Care should also be taken to avoid choosing weedy-looking ground cover for the front yard. Ground cover that matures over 8 inches in height may require a yearly mowing. Given that the lawn vigilante's vision becomes less acute as the winter season approaches, late blooming ground cover can be a judicious choice for the front yard. The backyard is a more democratic space and almost any variety of ground cover will suffice as long as some sections support light foot traffic.

Trees, subsequent to planting, are usually encircled by mulch. The ground cover should be set slightly back from the mulch and, should the mulch not be refreshed, the ground cover will gradually occupy the same space.

Roots

The roots of plants, and trees in particular, are of equal importance for the health of the environment as their aboveground structures. The entirety of a tree's water supply comes from its roots, the root systems of almost all trees can be found within the first 3 feet of soil, and these roots often extend two or three times farther than the spread of its crown. This means that, if the crowns of trees are relatively close, rather than overlapping or adjacent, the mere proximity of one tree to the other will ensure the interweaving of their root systems. Conjoined in the tree's roots are the

roots of the understory and herbaceous plants. This sharing of roots not only implies a sharing of resources but also the sharing of the mychorrhizal fungi mass that colonizes roots. As previously explained, mychorrhizal fungi provide plants, and trees in particular, with increased water and nutrient absorption capabilities.

3. TECHNIQUE

Given that the reader has completed the studies and tasks previously set forth, inclusive of selecting a satisfactory range of native plants and understanding their characteristics, it is now time to put tracing paper to the site plan and pencil to paper.

1. Start by reviewing your choices of native plants—their characteristics and sizes as well as your ideas for the paved space—secondary paths, and accessories. When the review is complete, make a legend for items that will be used to compose your sylvan landscape. Use different colors for the principal items. (An example of such a legend can be found in Chapter 9.)

2. If there are any trees, shrubs, or hardscape to be uprooted or demolished, align a piece of tracing paper over Site Plan A and redraw without the unwanted items.

3. Draw small heavy black dots, called registration marks, in each of the four corners of the final site plan (A or B). Copy these marks on each fresh sheet of tracing paper. This way, as long as the dots on the tracing paper align with the dots on the site plan, each successive overlay will be perfectly aligned.

4. Begin with the hardscape: Align a first piece of tracing paper over the site plan and draw a rough outline of where you feel the paved space could be and to where or from where the secondary paths should lead, such as back doors, pollinator garden, birdbath (a must), compost pit, and other places. Existing trees in the backyard will be a strong factor in all these decisions.

5. Trees: The position of the new trees will be informed by any existing trees' size and situation. Without getting too involved in measuring the diameters of trunks, three or four small to medium-sized trees for every large tree is a good grouping. The crowns of the new trees, at maturity, should not overhang the house; however, they can modestly overhang the property boundaries. Align a second piece of tracing paper over the first and draw circles, of a size roughly equivalent to the trees' canopies at 20 years of age.

6. Shrubs: Align a third piece of tracing paper over the first two and draw overlapping ovals, roughly the size of grown and trimmed shrubs.

7. Ground cover: Align a fourth piece of tracing paper over the first three and position the ground cover.

    (At this juncture, it is more than probable that some or all of the tracing paper visions need adjustments. If so, remove and replace individual sheets until your landscape design has been refined.)

8. When the positions of all the plants and hardscape have been finalized, copy the final results onto a fresh copy of the site plan and assign a unique number to each species of plants in the landscape. This finished design is referred to as a bubble diagram. (Examples of completed bubble diagrams are in Chapter 9.)

CHAPTER 7

At Home with Nature

"In Xanadu did Cublai Kahn build a stately Palace, encompassing sixteen miles of plaine ground with a wall, wherein are fertile Meddowes, pleasant Springs, delightful Streames, and all sorts of beasts of chase and game, and in the midst thereof a sumptuous house of pleasure, which may be moved from place to place."
—*Purchas his Pilgrimes* (1614), Samuel Purchas

TRADITIONAL CHINESE landscape design refers to the landscape construction activity and related representative works beginning with the Yin Shang dynasty and going to the end of the Qing Dynasty, a period of almost 4,000 years.[*] Europeans, in their accounts and descriptions of Chinese gardens, outlined these gardens' inherent characteristics, as distinct from western gardens. What westerners considered to be the natural appearance of a Chinese garden implied an irregularity of form, whereas this seeming irregularity was entirely calculated by the Chinese landscapers as an artifice intended to evoke the simplicity of a natural landscape. Occasionally this result was achieved through a concentration of a few elements, sometimes in rather tiny areas, but nature's multifaceted appearance was always evoked through diversification of the garden's aspects. From the Chinese we deduce:

- The garden should represent the superior natural order that humans belong to and that it is right to submit to, at least while in the garden.

- The paths through the landscape are important scenery lines, not only because they have the function of bearing foot traffic, but also the purpose of organizing scenery and inviting travel through the garden.

The *Iliad* and *The Odyssey* were the West's first and most perfect written works.[**] Homer, the commonly acknowledged author of both, references sacred groves—culturally charged landscapes used for worship—with epithets such as "rich in trees" and "shadow-spreading." Three centuries later, the emerging Greek city-states built temples around these sacred groves. Today, visiting the ruins of these temples, one still finds old trees, carefully fenced in by antique walls against goats and sheep, their interiors a haven for sweet smelling shrubs and wildflowers. An ancient Greek proverb, one that lends credence to the abundant use of trees in a sylvan landscape, says the following: A society grows great when old men plant trees whose shade they know they will never sit in. From the Greeks we deduce:

- Trees are sacred, ripeness is all.

[*] Encompassing the ancient Chinese art of geomancy and the more recent *fengshui* of wind and water.
[**] The *Iliad* and *The Odyssey* are dated somewhere between the 7th and 8th centuries BC.

Leonardo da Vinci, the quintessential visionary of the High Italian Renaissance,[*] was a practicing painter who made many of his scientific observations through the prism of painting. Leonardo's vision was particularly acute when it came to the proportions of trees in a landscape, and he famously observed that "all the branches of a tree at every stage of its height when put together are equal in thickness to the trunk," a simple yet startling one-to-one relationship between the diameter of a tree's trunk and the diameters of its branches. Leonardo da Vinci's Rule of Branches, as his observation came to be called, although aimed at instructing the apprentice painter, does make it easier for the landscaper to visualize the mass of a tree's crown, hence its proportion and scale vis-à-vis the landscape. In landscaping, proportion refers to the size of the landscape elements in relation to each other and to the design as a whole, whereas scale refers to the size of the landscape elements in relation to their inert surroundings. From the Italians we deduce:

- The landscape should be designed to accommodate the greatest number of trees that the size of the property will permit, with more smaller trees than large ones.

Darwinians think of trees as striving, disconnected loners, competing for water, nutrients, and sunlight, with the winners shading out the losers and sucking them dry. When the neighboring trees die, gaps open up in the protective forest canopy, and with an increased supply of water and sunlight the lone tree can photosynthesize more sugar and grow faster. While a big tree, standing by itself, may look majestic and self-reliant, it is lost and near-useless to the environment. Moreover, if the law of natural selection supposes that trees should be competing, why should one tree share resources with another? Apparently, it does not make evolutionary sense for any tree to hog the available resources; the strongest would eventually be isolated, and the lone tree is more vulnerable to the elements, diseases, and other dangers than its communal brethren and often dies before its time. This is why trees in stable forests live longer and reproduce better than their isolated scions. There is a substantial and growing body of scientific evidence that refutes the Darwinist approach and recognizes that trees form alliances with other trees and can put up a unified defense against danger. For example, when under attack from insects, bark-eating animals, or disease, some trees release distress chemicals—pheromones—into the air that can blunt or hinder the attack. These same pheromones cause other trees to emit similar pheromones, the conclusion being that trees have evolved to live in cooperative biorelationships that safeguard the health of all plant members. From the scientists we deduce:

- Trees enjoy the company of other trees.

Enclosure comes from the French "enclos," meaning "that which is closed in," and it is a term often used in reference to closed gardens. From these humble beginnings, American landscape architects have chosen to adhere to one of the more baffling of landscaping theories, the Law of Significant Enclosure. Of English or American origin, this now widely quoted law rests upon a precise mathematical formulae for the height of walls that will heighten humans' sense of well-being: "a person feels enclosed when the vertical edge of a space is at least one-third the length of the horizontal space."

[*]   Most art historians agree that the High Italian Renaissance started around 1495 or 1500 and ended in 1520 with the death of Raphael.

If applied to the average suburban plot, the law could only apply to the backyard and would seem to require a rather robust outer wall. To venture deeper into the current sea of landscape philosophies, hoping to extract elements applicable to sylvan landscaping, would be a chilling experience, as these modern disciplines have complex rules and laws that must be digested, followed, or ignored. There are, for example, the Seven Principles of Simplicity, which dictate the importance of variety, balance, emphasis, sequence, scale, and unity. The principles of the Golden Mean and the Golden Rectangle regulate proportions. Other curious rules stress that size matters, lines regulate, and opposites exclude. As sylvan landscaping is an innately ephemeral art, much of the above can be ignored. From the Anglo-Saxons we deduce:

- A sense of well-being can be afforded by a sense of enclosure.

Recent green thought has endowed trees with higher faculties than previously imagined, positing that trees in community form a social network wherein they intentionally communicate with each other. Some enthusiasts have ventured to postulate that trees have a consciousness not unlike creatures of the animal kingdom or even our own. The thought is that trees, when planted in community, will not only consult with one another to better outfox the elements, but will enjoy classical music and bond with their temporal custodians. Shrubs, ground cover, and wildflowers, if size and longevity are not determinate factors, are reputed to add to this discourse. To delve deep into plant consciousness theory is to chase a delightful sidetrack. From the sensitive among us we deduce:

- Trees should be planted close enough to one another so that, at maturity, their root systems will have intermingled and hopefully encircled the house. Because tree roots can extend to at least twice the size of their canopy, they will delve under any primary paths or hardscape.
- Shrub-rows should be planted in organic lines with regard for the outlines of the tree canopies.
- The paved space should emerge from the interstices of paths.

Mutatis mutandis is a Latin phrase that has crept (slowly) into the English language and means "with things changed that should be changed," similar to the more common "without loss of generality." In tune with the above-listed elements, *mutatis mutandis* would be the leitmotif of sylvan landscaping, iterating on nature with the property at hand.

CHAPTER 8

Envisioning a Sylvan Landscape at Maturity

Lo! in the middle of the wood,
The folded leaf is woo'd from out the bud
With winds upon the branch, and there
Grows green and broad, and takes no care,
Sun-steep'd at noon, and in the moon
Nightly dew-fed; and turning yellow
Falls, and floats adown the air.
Lo! sweeten'd with the summer light,
The full-juiced apple, waxing over-mellow,
Drops in a silent autumn night.
All its allotted length of days
The flower ripens in its place,
Ripens and fades, and falls, and hath no toil,
Fast-rooted in the fruitful soil.
—*The Lotos-Eaters* (1832), Alfred, Lord Tennyson

A SPACE IS SAID to have a "sense of place" if it has a strong identity that is deeply felt by inhabitants and visitors. Sense of place is a social phenomenon wherein a space has been ordered to serve some human need. Areas that lack a sense of place are often regarded as "placeless" or "inauthentic." Developers, in deference to a "sense of place," often gift their developments with a thematic veneer that recalls the distinctive features of the landscape that was erased during construction. Naming the community after the long-gone sylvan idyll it replaced, developers gain considerable purchase from a sense of nostalgia, coupled with the aristocratic pretensions that turf-grass lawns pretend to bestow. From this sad ending it follows that suburban beauty does not lie in the eye of the beholder but rather in the deception of developers.

At maturity, a sylvan landscape can restore a sense of place to a suburban property, and its singular identity will have come from the homeowner's collaboration with nature. Ten years is a safe estimate for the beginning of said maturity, but what will it look like? Given any one region's vast array of native plants and the nation's modest array of suburban tract configurations, the possible sylvan landscaping designs are near infinite. Yet, once the plants for the design have been chosen, the shapes of trees and shrubs, as well as the impact of pruning upon each, can be reasonably ascertained from books, online articles, visits to plant nurseries, arboretums, etc. By such means it is possible to form an idea of what each plant, and therefore the landscape, will look like when mature.

The following exercises are to give homeowners a first opportunity to envision what a property similar to their own, fully landscaped with regional native plants, would look like at maturity. While each exercise comes with a different property configuration, all respect the essence of sylvan landscaping: the use of a large number of trees with a higher proportion of smaller trees to the larger; shrub-rows placed at the edges of the tree's crowns; and curved secondary paths that connect the paved space with the landscape.

As all the properties in the exercises are imaginary, the shapes of the lots, houses, and primary paths have been simplified for the sake of illustration. The crown sizes of the trees are 20-year estimates. All plants are numbered sequentially, starting with trees, then shrubs, then ground cover and wildflowers. In order to make every exercise useful to every homeowner, the author has also completed every exercise, each for a different region, replete with some useful photos, a short review of potential wildlife visitors, and a nut and berry survey.

The homeowner should: (first) review all six designs, (second) choose a design that best resembles their own property, and (third) populate the design with plants native to their region. The exercise is like painting with numbers, except the coloring is done with plants. Also to be considered are the needs of the local wildlife, as well as nuts, fruits, and berries of household interest.

EXERCISE #1: HARTFORD, CONNECTICUT
DESCRIPTION OF THE PROPERTY

The lot (95 feet x 115 feet = 10,350 square feet) is rectangular and flat. The house has a footprint of 1,200 square feet and faces east. The primary paths cover 300 square feet. There are neighbors on all three sides.

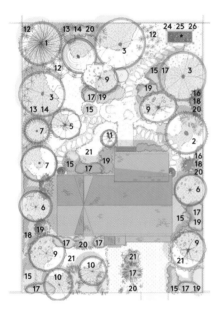

TREES
1. American basswood
2. Shagbark hickory
3. Red maple
4. Cherry birch
5. Common persimmon
6. American holly
7. Mountain maple
8. Red mulberry
9. Flowering dogwood
10. Eastern redbud
11. Ginkgo

SHRUBS
12. Highbush blueberry
13. Southern arrowwood
14. American hazelnut
15. Black chokeberry
16. Maple-leaf viburnum
17. Virginia rose
18. Buttonbush
19. Evergreen inkberry
20. Mountain laurel

GROUND COVER
21. Partridgeberry
22. Barren strawberry
23. Wild ginger

WILDFLOWERS
24. Milkweed
25. Butterfly weed
26. Wild red columbine

*COMPOST

Mutatis Mutandis

To evoke sensibility in the mind of the designer, the contours of the land to be shaped should be like musical notes rising and falling amid expectant silences. Absent such trills, a flat and featureless terrain, like a blank canvas, depends solely upon the artist's brush. Here are the first broad strokes:

HARDSCAPE: The paved space has been placed in the middle of the backyard, closer to the house rather than the street, with three curved paths pinwheeling around it: one on the left leading almost to the front yard, one on the right leading past the back door and the side; and the center path leading past a birdbath toward a pollinator garden and compost pit. A bench toward the back of the front yard adds interest.

TREES: The backyard contains five larger trees of three varieties, evenly spaced along the backsides of the property. These large trees provide focal points for those looking out from the paved space, The backyard has room for nine smaller trees of various varieties, spaced between the larger trees and the paved space, and extending into the side yards. Due to its small size, only smaller trees have been used in front yards, preferably species that could be pruned to have multiple trunks that favor larger crowns.

SHRUBS: The abundance of trees requires an equal abundance of shrub-rows and a variety of shrub species; in this instance, there are some 40-plus shrubs of 10 different kinds.

GROUND COVER AND WILDFLOWERS: A single species of ground cover that will accommodate light foot traffic should be used for the entire front yard as well as the center area around the paved space. The ground cover on the sides and back can have more of a vertical profile. The wildflowers behind the compost pit are for pollinators.

NORTHEASTERN SYLVAN LANDSCAPE

TREES: (1) Basswood: *Tilia Americana*; (2) Shagbark hickory: *Carya ovea*; (3) Red maple: *Acer rubra*; (4) Cherry birch: *Betula lenta*; (5) Common persimmon: *Diospyros virginiana*; (6) American holly: *Ilex opaca*; (7) Mountain maple: *Acer spicatem*; (8) Red mulberry: *Morus rubra*; (9) Flowering dogwood: *Cornus florida*;

AMERICAN BASSWOOD

SHAGBARK HICKORY

(10) Eastern redbud: *Cercis canadaenis*;
(11) Gingko: *Gingko bilboa* (a non-native of con-servation concern).

SHRUBS: (12) Highbush blueberry: *Vaccinium corymbosum*; (13) Southern arrowwood: *Viburnam dentate*; (14) American hazelnut: *Corylus Americana*; (15) Black chokeberry: *Aronia melanpcarpa*; (16) Maple-leaf vibur-num: *Viburnum acerifolium*; (17) Virginia rose: *Rosa Virginia*; (18) Common buttonbush: *Caphalanthus occidentalis*; (19) Evergreen inkberry: *Ilex glabda*; (20) Mountain laurel: *Kalmia latifolia*.

GROUND COVERS AND WILDFLOWERS:
(21) Partridgeberry: *Mitchella repens*; (22) Bar-ren strawberry: *Waldsteinia fragariodes*;
(23) Wild ginger: *Asarum canadense*; (24) Com-mon milkweed: *Asclepias syriaca*; (25) Butterfly weed: *Ascleoias tuberosa*; (26) Wild red colum-bine: *Aquilegia Canadensis*.

Potential Wildlife Visitors

EASTERN CHIPMUNK: A small rodent found in the eastern states that can reach a length of about 8 inches, one-third of which is its tail. The name chipmunk comes from the Algon-quin word meaning "one who descends trees headlong." Indeed, the eastern chipmunk, who has 4 toes each on the front legs and 5 on the back, does climb down trees headfirst but, less dexterously, prefers to live in complex underground nests with extensive tunnel sys-tems. The chipmunk is mostly active during the day, spending the bulk of its time foraging for food.

FROM TOP: Eastern redbud; Highbush blueberry; Wild ginger

"Eastern Chipmunk"

BLACK-THROATED BLUE WARBLER: A small, midnight-blue migratory songbird that is supposed to mate for life (see illustration on page 11). Like so many of its fellow New Englanders, the monogamous black-throated blue warbler breeds in the northeastern states and winters in the Caribbean. Another similarity, discreetly called "extra-pair mating," is when the male blue warblers cheat on their spouses. As expected, the blue warbler requires a mature forest with a dense understory for such breeding purposes. Warblers are predominantly insectivorous but will supplement their Caribbean diet with berry, seed, and fruit coladas.

AMERICAN CROW: A large omnivorous bird, found in every state, with iridescent black feathers, bill, and feet, that measures about 20 inches in length, 40% of which is tail. The American

"American crow"

crow is one of only a few species of birds that has been observed modifying and using tools to obtain food. Besides its intelligence, the American crow is also a very useful bird, but its somber coloring and hoarse voice has given it an undeserved bad reputation. James Audubon,[*] a painter and naturalist, was sympathetic to the crow's plight: "The crow is an extremely shy bird, having found familiarity with man no way to his advantage. He is also cunning—at least he is so called, because he takes care of himself and his brood. The state of anxiety, I may say of terror, in which he is constantly kept, would be enough to spoil the temper of any creature."

GREEN LACEWING: A winged insect found in every state and characterized by a wide costal field with crossveins in their wing ventilation. Adult green lacewings have tympanal organs at the base of their forewings, enabling them to hear well and commence evasive behavior when they hear a bat's ultrasound calls. If a green lacewing hears a bat while flying, it closes its wings, reducing its echolocational signature, and drops to the ground. Lacewing larvae are vicious and carnivorous, often described as

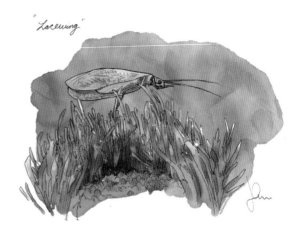

resembling tiny alligators, and are popularly known as ant lions.

Nature's Gifts for the Table, Larder, and Apothecary

Nuts from the shagbark hickory and American hazelnut. Fruits, berries, jellies, and pies from the persimmon, mayhaw, red mulberry, serviceberry, highbush blueberry, and black chokeberry. Brews, oils, and medicines from the basswood, evergreen inkberry, and wild ginger.

[*]   *The Birds of America*, plate 156 (1838), John James Audubon.

EXERCISE #2: ATLANTA, GEORGIA
DESCRIPTION OF THE PROPERTY

The lot (75 feet x 115 feet = 8,300 square feet) is long, thin, and rectangular, and it has a truncated back left corner. The house faces due south, has a raised open porch on its left side, and makes a footprint of 1,325 square feet. The primary paths cover 800 square feet. The downward sloping terrain in the back right has been leveled with a small south-facing retaining wall. There are neighbors on the left and right sides.

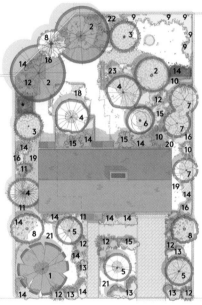

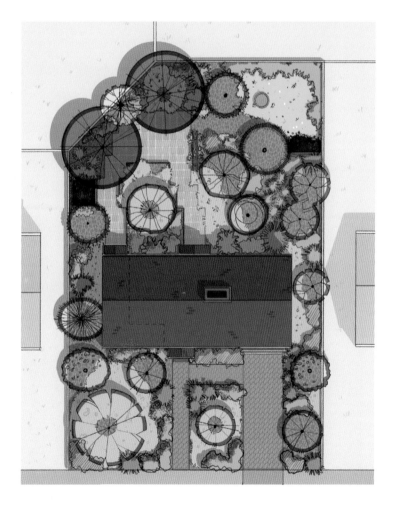

TREES
1. Southern magnolia
2. Pin oak
3. American yellowwood
4. American hornbeam
5. Grancy graybeard
6. Downy serviceberry
7. Mayhew
8. Washington hawthorn

SHRUBS
9. Red buckeye
10. American beauty-berry
11. Sweetshrub
12. Strawberrybush
13. Dwarf fothergilla
14. Oakleaf hydrangea
15. Winterberry
16. Drooping leucothoe

VINES AND GROUND COVER
17. Wisteria
18. Heartleaf foam-flower
19. Green-and-fold
20. Pennsylvania sedge
21. Dwarf smilax

WILDFLOWERS
22. Clasping milkweed
23. White milkweed
24. Wildflower mix

Mutatis Mutandis

The salient but contrasting features of the property are the truncated left corner and the raised back right corner.

HARDSCAPE: A paved space was constructed with medium-sized to large flagstones nestled in between the front edges of the trees in the truncated corner and joined visually with the raised corner via a pergola. The secondary paths connect the back door to the porch, the paved space, and compost pit.

TREES: There is only space for a single large tree, leaving ample room for a half-dozen smaller trees that can stretch around the sides to give the porch some privacy. The paved space has a large tree at each of its four corners interspersed with another half-dozen smaller trees.

SHRUBS: The shrub-rows in front are placed to provide shelter for the ground cover. The shrub-rows in the back are positioned to further privatize the paved space and to not obstruct the view from the raised porch. The back right corner has three to four shrubs pruned up to the size of a small tree to provide a windbreak for a small wildflower garden.

GROUND COVER AND WILDFLOWERS: As will often be the case with front yards, a ground-hugging ground cover is advised. A flowering ground cover near the wildflower garden would be nice. The pergola needs a vine.

SOUTHEASTERN SYLVAN LANDSCAPE

TREES: (1) Southern magnolia: *Magnolia grandiflora*; (2) Willow oak: *Quercus phellos*; (3) American yellowwood: *Claudrastis kentuckea*; (4) American hornbeam: *Carpius carolniana*;

WILLOW OAK

SOUTHERN MAGNOLIA

AMERICAN HORNBEAM

CLOCKWISE FROM TOP LEFT: Southern magnolia; American beautyberry; Green-and-gold; American yellowwood
OPPOSITE: Dwarf fothergilla

(5) Grancy graybeard: *Chionanthus virginicus*;
(6) Downy serviceberry: *Amelanshier arborea*;
(7) Mayhaw: *Crataegus aestivalis*; (8) Washington hawthorn: *Crataegus phaeneopyrum*.

SHRUBS: (9) Red buckeye: *Aesculus pavia*;
(10) American beautyberry: *Callicarpa Americana*; (11) Sweetshrub: *Calycanthus floridus*;
(12) Strawberry bush: *Euonymus gardenia*;
(13) Dwarf fothergilla: *Fothergilla gardenia*;
(14) Oakleaf hydrangea: *Hydrangea quadrifolia*; (15) Winterberry: *Ilex verticillata*;
(16) Rabbiteye blueberry: *Vaccinium viratom*

VINES, GROUND COVER, AND WILDFLOWERS:
(17) American wisteria: *Wisteria frutescens*;
(18) Heartleaf foamflower: *Tiarelle cordifolia*;
(19) Green-and-gold: *Chrysogonum virginianum*;
(20) Pennsylvania sedge: *Carex pensylvavica*;
(21) Dwarf smilax: *Smilax pumilla*; (22) Clasping milkweed: *Asclepias amplexicaulis*; (23) White milkweed: *Asclepias varigata*; (24) Georgia wildflower mix. (Georgia's Botanical Garden Society has developed a wildflower seed mix with southeastern pollinators in mind.)

Potential Wildlife Visitors

EASTERN GRAY SQUIRREL: A rodent native to states east of the Rockies. The most ecologically essential natural forest regenerator. The eastern gray squirrel's scientific name alludes to the squirrel sitting in the shade of its tail, which is large, gray, bushy, and about the same length as its body. The gray squirrel is a scatter hoarder, meaning it hoards food in numerous small caches for later recovery. A single gray squirrel is estimated to make several thousand caches each season and has an accurate spatial memory that allows it to retrieve the hidden food. Gray squirrels are crepuscular, meaning they are more active during the early and late hours of the day and do not hibernate.

BARN OWL: A medium-sized nocturnal predator that has long wings and a short, squared tail, found in every continent except Antarctica. The barn owl relies on its acute sense of hearing, rather than its sight, when hunting small mammals in the dark. Able to fly silently, thanks to its specialized feathers, barn owls do not hoot, but rather emit an eerie, drawn-out, unsettling shriek that has earned these useful creatures the undeserved epithets of "demon owl" and "ghost owl." Barn owls mate for life unless one of the pair is killed and a new pair bond is formed.

BALTIMORE ORIOLE: A medium-sized migratory songbird common to the eastern states. Baltimore orioles forage for insects and berries but have a preference for berries that are dark colored and ripe. Like hummingbirds, orioles lap up berry juices and nectars with their long tongues. Elm trees, prior to their decimation by Dutch elm disease, were the preferred nesting sites for Baltimore orioles. But these colorful birds have adapted, and their distinctive bag-shaped nests, artfully woven of plant fibers, can be seen hanging from many species of deciduous shade trees.

SOUTHEASTERN BLUEBERRY BEE: A winged insect regarded as the most efficient pollinator of the southern rabbiteye blueberry bush. Some species of blueberry bushes require buzz pollination, where vibrations from the bee's buzzing causes the pollen to shake loose. The blueberry bee is one of the species of bees that exhibit buzz behavior. Southwestern blueberry bees are active for only a few weeks in the early spring when the blueberries are in flower. The southern blueberry is a busy bee, and it is estimated that an adult female can visit up to 40,000 blueberry flowers in a single season.

Nature's Gifts for the Table, Larder, and Apothecary

Fruits, berries, jellies, and pies from the downy serviceberry, mayhaw, rabbiteye blueberry, and Washington hawthorn. Brews, oils, and medicines from the American beautyberry, sweetshrub, strawberry bush, and heartleaf foamflower.

EXERCISE #3: ST. LOUIS, MISSOURI
DESCRIPTION OF THE PROPERTY

The lot (80 feet x 100 feet = 8,000 square feet) is small and nearly square. The house straddles a small rise in the terrain close to the front, has a footprint of 1,300 square feet, and faces due south. The primary paths cover 475 square feet. Both the front and backyards drain well. There are neighbors on all three sides.

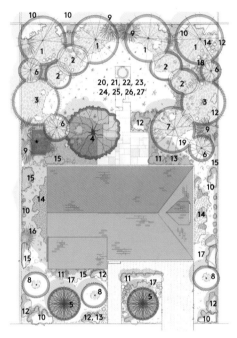

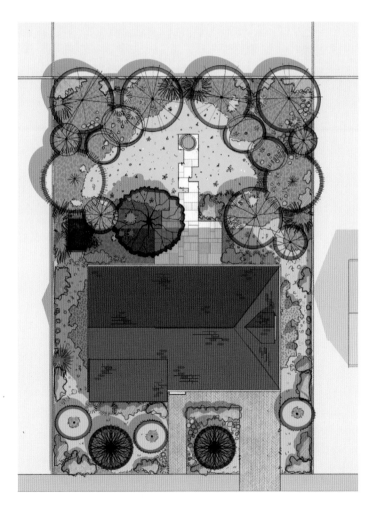

TREES
1. Shortleaf pine
2. River birch
3. Hardy Pecan
4. Sugarberry
5. Kentucky coffeetree
6. Chinquapin
7. Black gum
8. Crabapple

SHRUBS
9. Smoketree
10. Deciduous holly
11. Roseshell azaela
12. Vernal witch hazel
13. Wild hydrangea
14. Blackberry
15. American snowbell

GROUND COVER
16. Wild petunia
17. Sand flox
18. False Rue anemone
19. Buffalo Grass

WILDFLOWERS
20. Little bluestem
21. Missouri Black-eyed Susan
22. Prairie coneflower
23. Butterfly milkweed
24. Purple prairie clover
25. Missouri primrose
26. Pasture rose
27. Spider milkweed

*COMPOST

Mutatis Mutandis

The larger open space in the center of the backyard framed by trees suggests the appearance of an edge, or the line where the forest meets the meadow. It is doubtful that such a feeble edge will increase the biodiversity of the backyard, but it is certain that the periodic burning of the meadow will raise hackles.

HARDSCAPE: As the backyard slopes after it passes the crowns of the large trees, the paved space needs to be close to the back door and near the shade and may as well begin just past the back door. A single secondary path toward the compost will suffice. A larger-than-average birdbath set between the meadow and paved space completes the tableau.

TREES: The centrist configuration of the house and the square lot resulted in a quasi-symmetrical setting of trees. The protective row of similar trees set across the back and sides of the lot faced by smaller trees creates the appearance of a forest behind the meadow. Two varieties of smaller trees in the front yard complement the quasi-symmetry of the backyard.

SHRUBS: The front and side yard shrubs should modestly highlight the trees, whereas the backyard shrubs privatize and shelter the meadow.

GROUND COVER AND WILDFLOWERS: The same ground cover in the front yard, at the edges, and cutting through the meadow should support the foot traffic necessary for the maintenance of each. Additionally, this same ground cover sections the meadow into different plots. As the meadow can accommodate a large selection of grasses and wildflowers, other ground covers should extend the metaphor.

MIDWESTERN SYLVAN LANDSCAPE

TREES: (1) Shortleaf pine: *Pinus echinata*; (2) River birch: *Betula nigra*; (3) Pecan: *Carya illinoinsis*; (4) Sugarberry: *Celyis laevigata*; (5) Kentucky coffee tree: *Gymnocladus dioicus*; (6) Allegheny chinquapin: *Castanea pumila*; (7) Black gum: *Nyssa sylvatica*; (8) Prairie crab apple: *Malus ioensis*.

TOP: Kentucky coffee tree
BOTTOM: Prairie crab apple

RIVER BIRCH

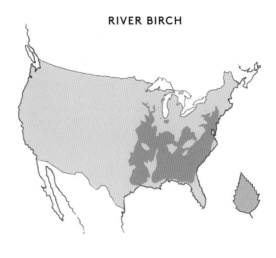

PECAN

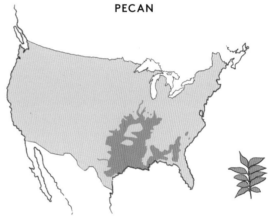

SHORTLEAF PINE

SHRUBS: (9) American smoketree: *Cotinus obovatus*; (10) Possumhaw holly: *Ilex decidua*; (11) Roseshell azalea: *Rhododendron prinophyllum*; (12) Vernal witch hazel: *Hamamelis vernalis*; (13) Wild hydrangea: *Hydrangea arborescens*; (14) Blackberry: *Rubus sp.*; (15) American snowbell: *Styrix americangus.*

GROUND COVER AND WILDFLOWERS: (16) Wild petunia: *Ruellia humilus*; (17) Sand phlox: *Phlox bifida*; (18) False rue anemone: *Isopyrum biternatum*; (19) Buffalo grass: *Bouteloua dactyloides*; (20) Little bluestem: *Schizachyrium scoparium*; (21) Missouri black-eyed Susan: *Rudbeckia missouriensis*; (22) Purple coneflower: *Echinacea purpurea*; (23) Purple milkweed: *Asclepias purpurascens*; (24) Purple prairie clover: *Palea purpurea*; (25) Missouri primrose:

TOP: Vernal witch hazel
BOTTOM: Roseshell azalea

CLOCKWISE FROM TOP: Missouri black-eyed Susan; Purple coneflower; Blackberry

Oenothera macrocarpa; (26) Pasture rose: *Rosa Carolina*; (27) Spider milkweed: *Asclepias viridis*.

Potential Wildlife Visitors

LITTLE BROWN BAT: A species of nocturnal, hibernating, mouse-eared mammal that weighs less than ½ oz. and is about 3 inches long. Bats are the only mammals capable of true flight. The little brown bat, called LBB by the naturalist, has glossy brown fur and employs a sophisticated system of echolocation to find its food, for the most part insects and spiders along the edges of vegetated habitat. The LBB is a colonial species, with hibernating colonies that can exceed 100,000 individuals. Eerily, the caves that bats use for hibernation are called hibernacula.

"Little Brown Bat"

EASTERN AMERICAN FOX: A medium-sized predator found in all states east of the Rocky Mountains except southern Texas. The preferred habitat of the eastern red fox is a mixed landscape made up of patches of forests, grasslands, and other land-use areas that provide edge. They adapt well to human presence and are widely held as a symbol of cunning.

NORTHERN CARDINAL: A midsized songbird that ranges throughout the mid-western and eastern states. The northern cardinal's common name, as well as its scientific name, refers to the cardinals of the Roman Catholic Church who wear distinctive red robes and red caps. A ground feeder, the northern cardinal's diet consists mainly of weed seeds, grains, and fruits, and will find food while by hopping through shrubs or around trees. Unlike their pious namesakes, northern cardinals mate for life and feed their young almost exclusively upon insects.

MONARCH BUTTERFLY: A winged migratory butterfly with distinctive black, orange, and white wing patterns. The annual migrations of North America's monarch butterflies are unique, as the monarch is the only butterfly known to make a two-way migration like birds do. Unlike other butterflies that can overwinter as larvae, pupae, or even as adults, monarchs cannot survive the cold winters of northern climates, and those east of the Rocky mountains overwinter in Mexico's Sierra Madre Mountains. Monarchs use a combination of air and thermal currents to travel long distances, some traveling as far as 3,000 miles to reach their destinations.

"Monarch butterfly"

Nature's Gifts to the Table, Larder, and Apothecary

Nuts from the pecan and Allegheny Chinquapin. Fruits, jellies, and pies, from the sugarberry, prairie crab apple, and blackberry bush. Brews, oils, and medicines from the Kentucky coffee tree, wild hydrangea, and purple coneflower.

"Northern Cardinal"

EXERCISE #4: HOUSTON, TEXAS
DESCRIPTION OF THE PROPERTY

The development was built on a 100-year floodplain* in an area subject to frequent flooding. The house was built on a rectangular lot (90 feet x 105 feet = 9,450 square feet). In response to past flooding, the terrain surrounding the house has been graded 2 feet higher, and the house raised until the ground floor was 18 inches above the grade, bringing it above the level of the 500-year floodplain. The house has a footprint of 1,200 square feet and faces east-southeast. The primary paths cover 275 square feet. There are low-lying neighbors on all three sides.

* An area where a 100-year flood event has a 1 in 100 chance of occurring.

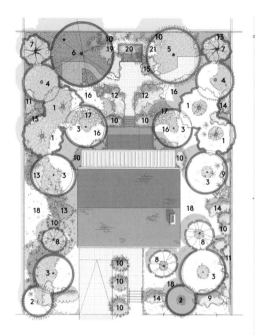

TREES
1. Bald cypress
2. Yaupon holly
3. Black willow
4. Water tupelo
5. Drummond's red maple
6. Southern live oak
7. Pepperwood
8. Mexican plum

SHRUBS
9. Coral berry
10. Texas lantana
11. Wax myrtle
12. Chile pequin
13. Roughleaf dogwood
14. Virginia sweetspire
15. Southern dewberry

GROUND COVER
16. Pigeonberry
17. Texas frogfruit
18. Powderpuff mimosa

POLLINATOR GARDENS
19. Antelope horns
20. Green milkweed
21. Texas milkweed

WILDFLOWER GARDEN
22. Texas Indian paintbrush
23. Texas bluebonnet
24. LBJ wildflower mix

*COMPOST

Mutatis Mutandis

Prevailing diluvian sediments* suggest that cattails and lily pads could be the best landscaping alternatives, for the soil is moist and does not drain well. Nor do the usual front and backyard distinctions accurately depict the spaces involved, whereas "island" and "off island" do. When the inevitable floods do come, the island will be able to keep the house dry as long as its edges have not eroded.

HARDSCAPE: Rather than a paved space, a slightly raised deck (6 inches) on the island—with guardrails and stairs heading offshore—was the best solution. The secondary paths begin at the bottom of the stairs and lead toward the compost pit in the back. A sturdy bench has been placed in the backyard so rescue boats could use it as an emergency mooring.

TREES AND SHRUBS: Put down roots, secure the edges of the island, and thwart soil erosion will be the overall strategy for all plants. Riparian species are suggested, both for the outer border of the island and the swamp lurking just below.

* Dating from the grounding of Noah's Ark.

GROUND COVER AND WILDFLOWERS:
Ground covers with matting roots, rather than the delving kind, are the best options, with a single species that supports foot traffic for the island.

GULF COAST SYLVAN LANDSCAPE

TREES: (1) Bald cypres: *Taxodium distichum Americana*; (2) Yaupon holly: *Ilex vomitoria*; (3) Black willow: *Salex nigra*; (4) Water tupelo: *Nyssa aquatica*; (5) Drummond's red maple: *Acer rubrum drummondii*; (6) Southern live oak: *Quercus virginiana*; (7) Pepperwood: *Zanthoxylum clava-herculis*; (8) Mexican plum: *Prunus Mexicana*.

SHRUBS: (9) Coral berry: *Symphoricarpos orbiculatus*; (10) Texas lantana: *Lantana urticoides*; (11) Wax myrtle: *Myrica cerifera*; (12) Chile pequin: *Capsicum frutscens*; (13) Roughleaf dogwood: *Cornua drummondii*; (14) Virginia sweetspire: *Itea virginica*; (15) Southern dewberry: *Rubrus trivialis*.

GROUND COVER AND WILDFLOWERS:
(16) Pigeonberry: *Rivinia humilis*; (17) Texas frogfruit: *Phyla nodiflora*; (18) Powderpuff mimosa: *Mimosa strigillosa*; (19) Antelope horns: *Acclepias asperule*; (20) Green milkweed: *Acclepias viridis*; (21) Texas milkweed: *Acclepias texana*; (22) Texas Indian paintbrush: *Castilleja indivisa*; (23) Texas bluebonnet: *Lupinus texensis*; (24) Lady Bird Johnson wildflower mix: *Caesar uxorem*.

Potential Wildlife Visitors

OPOSSUM: A semiarboreal omnivorous marsupial the size of a large domestic cat with an

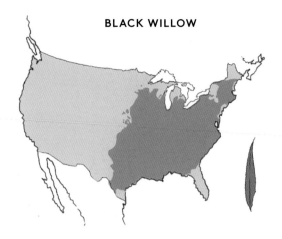

BLACK WILLOW

SOUTHERN LIVE OAK

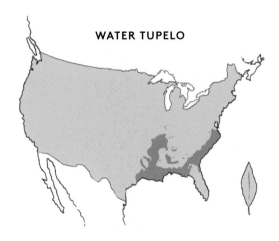

WATER TUPELO

OPPOSITE, CLOCKWISE FROM TOP LEFT: Bald cypress; Yaupon holly; Chile pequin; Texas bluebonnet; Texas lantana

Texas bluebonnet and Indian paintbrush

"Opossum"

opposable big toe, a naked tail, and 50 teeth. The Virginia opossum is the only native marsupial in North America. Originally from South America, "possums," as they are often called, came north when the two continents fused 300 million years ago. When Columbus arrived, the opossum's native range was in the southerly states east of the Rockies. Afterward, colonists introduced opossums into every state, primarily because they are good to eat. Opossums have unusually short life spans, perhaps due to intense predation or the ineffectiveness of pretending to be dead (playing possum) when threatened.

AMERICAN GOLDFINCH: A small, migratory songbird about the size of a stick of butter and generally monogamous. The American goldfinch lives at the edges between plains and forests in areas filled with brush and thistle plants. Given the goldfinch's preference for clearings and edge, the spread of suburbia has increased its numbers and range. American goldfinches are among the strictest vegetarians in the world, selecting an entirely vegetable diet. If

"American Goldfinch"

pings, have doubled the ratio of female frogs to males. Again, the act of maintaining a lawn can have dire consequences for wildlife. [**]

CONVERGENT LADYBUG: A useful beetle that is found in every state and that preys on aphids, scales, thrips, and other soft-bodied insects. Convergent ladybugs are easily recognized by their bright red or orange elytra (hardened forewings) that usually have 12 black spots, 6 per elytra. Ladybugs are often collected and sold to farmers and gardeners to help with pest control.

the parasitic cowbird[*] lays an egg in a goldfinch nest, the egg may hatch, but the unwanted nestling seldom survives longer than 3 days on the all-seed diet that goldfinches feed their young.

GREEN FROG: A midsized amphibian that can live wherever freshwater ponds, roadside ditches, lakes, swamps, streams, and brooks are found. While aquatic, the green frog will often go overland in search of food and is often found in the suburbs. By inhabiting an ecotone, in this case the terrestrial and aquatic habitat boundary, the green frog can sometimes escape its terrestrial enemies by hopping back into the water. An unfortunate result of the use of pesticides on suburban lawns and vegetable gardens is that these chemicals are disrupting the green frogs' endocrine systems, which, coupled with chemicals found in lawn clip-

"Ladybug"

Nature's Gifts to the Table, Larder, and Apothecary

Fruits, jellies, and/or pies, from the Mexican plum and southern dewberry. Oils, spices, and/or medicines from the pepperwood, wax myrtle, and chile pequin.

---

[*]   Cowbirds are brood parasites, laying their eggs in the nests of other species.
[**]   *Estrogen, shrubbery, and the sex ratio of suburban frogs*, Yale News (September 2015), Max Lambert, prof. Yale School of Forestry and Environmental Studies.

EXERCISE #5: SACRAMENTO, CALIFORNIA
DESCRIPTION OF THE PROPERTY

The rectangular lot (75 feet x 90 feet = 9,450 square feet) is flat and contains two structures: a house with a footprint of 1,485 square feet and a detached garage with a footprint of 179 square feet, both facing the rising sun. The primary paths cover 560 square feet. There are neighbors on all three sides whose houses and garages are similarly configured.

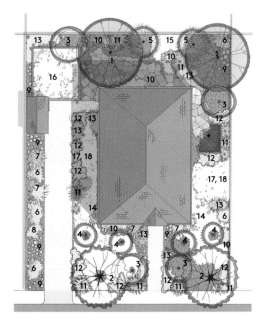

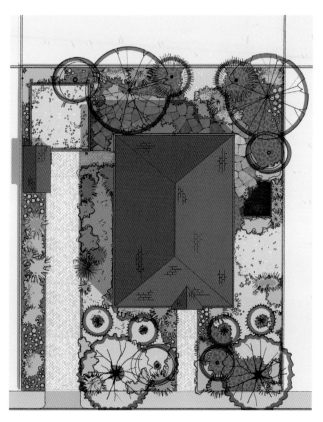

TREES
1. Valley oak
2. Black elm
3. Vine maple
4. Western redbud
5. California buckeye

SHRUBS
6. Deerbush
7. Buck brush
8. Hairy ceanothus
9. Lemmon's ceanothus
10. California allspice
11. California anemone
12. Oregon grape
13. California rose

GROUND COVER
14. Bearberry
15. Carpet manzanita
16. California wild grape

Poppy Garden
17. California poppy
18. Tufted poppy

*COMPOST

Mutatis Mutandis

The detached garage as well as the front and side yards' greater size than the backyard are features that can be exploited.

HARDSCAPE: Two-thirds of the large rectangular paved space has been placed under the branches on the sunny side of the large tree on the left and will provide afternoon choices of either shade or sun. The westerly facing house will shadow the paved space in the evening. A trellis on the south-facing wall of the garage can be garnished with vines to complete the sense of significant enclosure. The secondary paths connect the paved space with the garage, the side door, and the compost pit.

TREES: A large tree in each of the lot's four corners will shelter double the number of smaller trees interspersed throughout.

SHRUBS: A straight shrub-row, composed of related flowering species, almost like a fence, was used to fill in the long space to the left of the driveway. The shrubs have been planted in the middle of the strip so that they may be neatly trimmed on both sides. To a lesser degree, the other shrubs mimic fences.

VINES, GROUND COVER, AND WILDFLOWERS: The trellis on the south-facing wall of the garage will give three evenly spaced vines a chance to extend their reach across the front and back of the garage. As the abundance of primary and secondary paths allows egress to all spaces, simple treadworthy ground covers are suggested. The garden harbors showy, low-growing wildflowers.

WESTERN SYLVAN LANDSCAPE

TREES: (1) Valley oak (aka California white oak): *Quercus lobata*; (2) Black elm: *Ulmus Americana* (planted far from the blight that rages in the east); (3) Vine maple: *Acer circinatum*; (4) Western redbud: *Cercis occidentalis*; (5) California buckeye: *Aesculus californica*.

SHRUBS: (6) Deerbush: *Ceanothus integerrimus*; (7) Buck brush: *Ceanothus cuneatus*; (8) Hairy ceanothus: *Ceanothus oliganthus*; (9) Lemmon's ceanothus: *Ceanothus oliganthus*; (10) California allspice: *Calycanthus occidentalis*; (11) California anemone: *Carpenteria californica*.

VINES, GROUND COVERS, AND WILDFLOWERS: (12) Oregon grape: *Mahonia aquifolium*; (13) California rose: *Rosa californica*; (14) Bearberry: *Arctostaphylos uva-ursi*; (15) Carpet manzinita: *Arctostaphylos Emerald Carpet*; (16) California wild grape: *Vitus californica*; (17) California poppy: *Eschscholizia californica*; (18) Tufted poppy: *Eschscholizia caespitasa*; (19) Narrowleaf milkweed: *Asclepias fascicularis*.

Potential Wildlife Visitors

WESTERN COTTONTAIL: A smallish rabbit 14 to 17 inches long that ranges over the southwestern states. Unfortunately for the western cottontail, hopping down the bunny trail is not as carefree a pastime as it might sound, for almost every larger or faster carnivore, even snakes, line up along this fabled highway to prey upon rabbits. Highest on the bunny predator list is an invasive species, the common house cat, a domesticated ancestor of African and European

OPPOSITE, CLOCKWISE FROM TOP LEFT: Valley oak; California allspice; California poppy; Tufted poppy

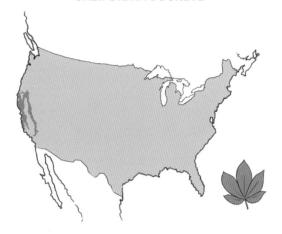

CALIFORNIA BUCKEYE

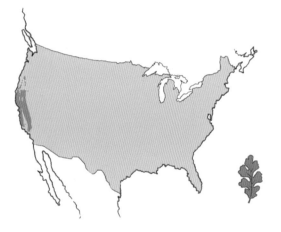

CALIFORNIA WHITE OAK

origin. As wind interferes with the cottontail's hearing and affects its ability to detect lurking predators, they rarely leave their burrows on windy days.

BOBCAT: A medium-sized feline in the lynx family that often reaches 40 inches in length, with tufted ears, spotted coat, and a short, bobbed tail. The bobcat hunts by stalking its prey and then ambushing with a short chase or pounce. As the bobcat targets mammals weighing less than 10 pounds, humans should not be

Mutatis Mutandis

A big house on a small property with too skinny side yards poses somewhat of an existential problem for a sylvan landscape.

HARDSCAPE: Some space and privacy were gained with a savant use of small fences along the back and sides. A compact geometric paved space, outfitted with permeable pavers rather than flagstones and connected to the back door also saves space. A single curved path to the birdbath and beyond is all the space will allow.

TREES: A large tree opposite the paved space, a medium-sized tree opposite the primary paths, and seven small trees scattered around are about all the property can take.

SHRUBS: A shrubbery along the front and sides takes over where the fences end, albeit those bordering the sidewalk should be trimmed lower than the fences. All the shrubbery in the backyard can be trimmed to the height or higher than the fences. The shrubbery around the paved space should be colorful.

VINES, GROUND COVER, AND WILDFLOWERS: The ground covers should hug the terrain but still impart a feeling of rusticity. The fences are all covered with climbing vines that could also encroach upon the shrubbery. A tiny pollinator garden will just fit in behind the compost pit.

NORTHWESTERN SYLVAN LANDSCAPE

TREES: (1) Western red cedar: *Thuja plicata*; (2) Red alder: *Alnus rubra*; (3) Pacific madrone: *Arbutus menziesii*; (4) Bigleaf maple: *Acer macrophyllum sericea*; (5) Black hawthorn: *Crataegus douglasii*.

SHRUBS: (6) Pacific rhododendron: *Rhododendron macrophyllum*; (7) Common juniper: *Juniperus communisus*; (8) Sitka mountain ash: *Sorbus sitchensis*; (9) Bitter cherry: *Prunus emarginata*; (10) Salal: *Gaultheria shallon*; (11) Baldhip rose: *Rosa gymnocarpa*.

VINES, GROUND COVER, AND WILDFLOWERS: (12) Trumpet honeysuckle: *Lonicera ciliosa*; (13) Pink honeysuckle: *Lonicera hispidula*; (14) Creeping dogwood: *Cornus canadensis*; (15) Twin flower: *Linnaea borealis*; (16) Showy milkweed: *Asclepias speciose*.

Potential Wildlife Visitors

RACCOON: A medium-sized nocturnal omnivore with extremely dexterous front paws, a facial mask, and a ringed tail. The raccoon's

WESTERN RED CEDAR

BIGLEAF MAPLE

"Raccoon"

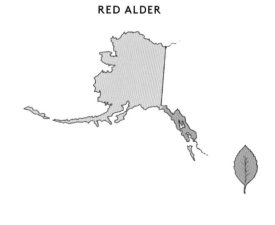

RED ALDER

Pacific madrone

natural habitat is deciduous and mixed forests, but due to its adaptability and intelligence it has extended its range into suburban and urban areas. Raccoons have vital urban skills: they can stand on their hind legs to examine food, swim, rotate their feet backward, climb down trees headfirst, and can survive falls of 25 feet. The most important sense for the raccoon is its sense of touch, and its dexterous paws can open water faucets for a drink or garbage cans for a snack.

WESTERN BLUEBIRD: A small migratory thrush that has been chased out of its natural habitat due to forestry. Notwithstanding the loss of much of its natural hardwood forest habitat, the western bluebird has adapted to coniferous forests and farmlands to survive. A cavity nester due to its weak beak, the tiny bluebird faces fierce competition for nesting sites from similarly inclined birds, particularly tree swallows,

house swallows, and the invasive European starling. Unfortunately, this new habitat poses yet another problem for the patient but suffer-

"Western Bluebird"

ing bluebird, this time in the form of parasites that attack its eggs. However, a recent study[*] indicates that a plentiful local food supply improves the eggs' resistance to parasites and specifically cites how suburban yards can help improve the bluebirds' habitat.

WESTERN SPOTTED OWL: A large predator that is a resident of old-growth forests in the Pacific Northwest. The western spotted owl seeks out dense canopy cover, and large trees in old-growth forests are their preferred nesting and roosting sites. Spotted owls are nocturnal, sit and wait for predators, and prefer to hunt from a perch where they can swoop or pounce on their prey. They may take arboreal prey, such as flying squirrels, from tree boles and limbs. Spotted owls do not build their own nests, instead making use of cavities found in trees, deadwood, and abandoned raptor or squirrel nests.

"Spotted Owl"

[*] *Journal of Applied Ecology,* University of Connecticut (2019), Sarah Knutie.

TOP TO BOTTOM: Pacific rhododendron, Salal, Red Alder

AMERICAN ROBIN: A medium-sized migratory songbird that ranges year-round in most every state. The American robin is an active feeder during the day and assembles in large flocks at night and roosts in trees. The flocks break up during the day when the individual birds feed or go bob-bob-bobbing along. The American robin is among the earliest of birds to lay its eggs and to sing at dawn. The male's song, as with many thrushes, is melodic, complex, and almost continuous.

FAMILIAR BLUET: A damselfly native to the northern states. Damselflies have much larger eyes than their dragonfly cousins. The familiar bluet is one of the brightest of blue damselflies, making them easy to spot as they dart from plant to plant looking for insects to eat. Because familiar bluets spend part of their life underwater, proximity to a water source is necessary to sustain a population, albeit they are not picky about home sites, even if they are muddy puddles formed after a hard rain.

Nature's Slim Pickings

Juniper berries are used to flavor gin. The leaves of the salal, chewed but not swallowed, are said to be an appetite suppressant.

"American Robin"

OPPOSITE, CLOCKWISE FROM TOP: Trumpet honeysuckle, Creeping dogwood, Twin flower

CHAPTER 9

Bringing Nature Home

> "The man who believes that the secrets of the world are forever hidden
> lives in mystery and fear. Superstition will drag him down. The rain will
> erode the deeds of his life. But the man who sets himself the task of
> singling out the thread of order from the tapestry will by the decision
> alone have taken charge of the world and it is only by taking such charge
> that he will effect a way to dictate the terms of his own fate."
> —*Blood Meridian* (1985), Cormac McCarthy

DESPITE CONCRETE EVIDENCE that should forever proscribe the use of turf grass in suburban yards, homeowners, before heeding *The Call of the Wild* and becoming masters of their own landscape, should perhaps consider the pecuniary aspects of aligning their property with nature. As this chapter will illustrate, the cost of installing a full sylvan landscape would be no more expensive than a traditional landscaping project, nor would the cost of maintaining it be higher, while mature trees add value to a property.* Turf grass, on the other hand, will wear out in about 20 years, or over the life spans of two decent power lawnmowers, and both must be replaced.

Reality imposes a sterner burden upon homeowners who decide to implement their design, for they must watch over and care for their chosen plants as they mature. For the rewards and benefits of a sylvan landscape are far greater than a toxic turf-grass lawn; they extend, in varying but just degrees, to the well-being of the inhabitants, the attendant wildlife, and the community.

BUDGET

The American Society of Landscape Architect's (ASLA) general rule for a full remake of a home's landscape is 10% to 20% of the home's value in consideration of the fact that landscape improvements return 100% to 200% of their cost if the house is sold.** Not unsurprisingly, ASLA also recommends the use of regional native plants to reduce watering and maintenance. If the value of the house is set at the US median, or $250,000, then a minimum budget for a major landscaping project, per the ASLA's reckoning, would be 10% of the home's value, or $25,000.

Wild harvesting of native plants is frowned upon for many good reasons and is impractical for many others. The most reliable sources for native plants are, unsurprisingly, native plant nurseries, particularly those whose plants have been grown from seed. However, almost every plant nursery will sell some native plants. Plant nurseries often offer land-

---

*   Healthy mature trees add an average of 10% to a property's value. USDA Forest Service.
**   ASLA.org.

"Eastern Bluebird"

"Staghorn Sumac"

scaping services or can arrange for such. For example, a native plant nursery that offers landscaping services will be referred to as a PN&L.

Ordering plants from a single PN&L, with the cost of delivery and planting included in the price, is the most cost-effective method, albeit one that can be beset by seasonal considerations and availability of desired specimens. Regional native plants are often less expensive than non-natives or cultivars. Then there is the question of what size plants to buy, as a larger plant is more expensive than a smaller plant of the same variety. Yet, buying a larger plant is like buying time, not just the time it took for the PN&L to grow the plant to that size, but also their investment in care and pruning. Bigger plants are also harder to transport and replant. While all plants will need water and extra care to help get established after replanting, a plant with

a bigger root system may have an easier time of it. On the other hand, a smaller plant may well adapt better to replanting, grow faster, and catch up to the bigger plant sooner rather than later.

The six examples of sylvan design in the preceding chapter contained an average of 16 trees, 30 shrubs, 5,000 square feet of ground cover, and 150 square feet of paved space. Using these numbers, the following estimates are based on an average price for reasonably sized plants purchased from a single PN&L.

Trees

Mature trees are expensive, young trees less so, and seedlings are cheap. For the purposes of this exercise, all trees will be taken to have been purchased in 15-gallon containers, are 2 to 3 years old, and are between 4 and 6 feet tall. Trees in this category can cost between $75 and $200 if picked up and planted by the buyer. If the PN&L delivers and installs the tree, which is recommended, the cost could be doubled. Installation usually includes digging the hole, removal of excess subsoil, planting, adding soil as necessary, and staking if required. If the homeowner's purchase is for multiple trees, there can be substantial discounts. As 16 trees, inclusive of planting, is a large order for a suburban property, $150 per tree is a reasonable estimate. The cost of 16 trees at $150 per tree = **$2,400.**

Shrubs

The optimal size for purchasing a shrub is in a 5-gallon container with costs ranging from $20 to $30 per shrub. Again, delivery and installation can double the price. As 30 shrubs, inclusive of planting, is a large order, $40 per shrub is a reasonable estimate. The cost of 30 shrubs at $40 per shrub = **$1,200.**

Ground Cover

A cost of $1.25 per square foot covers the cost of most ground covers as well as their installation. The cost of ground cover for 5,000 square feet at $1.25 per square feet = **$6,250.**

Paved Space

The cost to install stone paving is between $15 to $20 per square feet. Natural stone paving can cost from $40 to $70 per square feet. Taking the higher figure for the stone pavers, and the lower figure for the natural stone, an elegant, paved space in tune with the new landscape could cost around $45 per square feet. The cost of 150 square feet of paved space = **$6,750.**

Mulch

One cubic yard of mulch covers about 100 square feet at 3 inches deep, or 300 square feet at 1 inch deep. Three inches is the right depth for the secondary paths = 5 cubic yards of mulch. Two inches will be needed to protect the tree and roots = 2 cubic yards of mulch. The cost of 8 cubic yards of good-quality organic mulch, delivered and spread, would cost about $90 per cubic yard = **$720.**

Total Estimated Cost of Plants and Landscaping

The total estimated cost of plants and hardscape, per the above calculations, comes to **$17,340,** a little over 8% of $200,000. If more budget money is available, per ASLA's recommendation, it could be used to replace exposed concrete and asphalt driveways and walkways with pavers, which stay cooler, look better, and can be placed to allow vegetation to grow through.

* According to EPA statistics.

MAINTENANCE

Traditional versus Sylvan Landscape

During the first 3 years after executing a sylvan landscape design, the cost—measured in time and dollars—of maintaining the landscape would be more or less equal to the cost of maintaining a traditional landscape. By the third or fourth year, once the native plants have established themselves, the cost of maintaining a sylvan landscape will decline, while the cost of maintaining a turf-grass landscape will remain the same. The added cost arises from the constant mowing (gasoline and lawnmower maintenance), as well as the use of chemicals (fertilizers, herbicides, pesticides), irrigation, and waste removal that are all required to keep the lawn up to standard. The cost of water can only rise as this precious resource grows scarce and the nation's waste disposal systems are annually clogged by some 34.7 million tons of yard trimmings.[*]

The cost of fully outsourcing the maintenance of a traditional landscape to a sylvan landscape on a regular weekly basis would seem to be more or less equal per week, as the former requires weekly care and the latter requires more intensive care at bimonthly intervals.

Although a sylvan landscape, by using space as nature does, needs less human management to stay healthy, it still requires pruning and trimming to protect the health and to direct the growth of its plants. Pruning is performed in order to shape and protect the tree or shrub. Trimming is performed to ensure the perfect growth of the shrubs. It has been argued that as plants are not trimmed or pruned in the wild there is no need to do so in the yard. But this is not so, as the yard is not a fully unaltered segment of the natural world but rather a managed environment where selected plants are grown for specific effects. While it takes a higher degree of skill to prune a tree or shrub than it does to trim one, gaining that necessary degree of skill to do both is well within a homeowner's reach, and the reward is a greater degree of interest, particularly in comparison to the dull task of mowing.

While fall's leaves are anathema to a turf-grass lawn, they are a blessing to a natural landscape. Leaf litter plays an important part in natural processes, as nutrients in the leaves that fall each season are equivalent to three-fourths of the nutrients the tree took in during the year. The leaves that fall upon evergreen shrubs will slip off and land on the plants' roots, and the leaves that fall upon deciduous shrubs will fall to the plants' roots alongside the leaves from the shrubs. Higher quantities of leaf litter hold higher humidity levels, a key factor for the establishment of plants. As such, it is not necessary to compost all the fallen leaves, as they can be raked beneath the shrubs as a blanket that keeps the soil from washing away and exposing delicate feeder roots, resulting in better looking and healthier shrubs as well as more fertile soil. Many species of wildlife also depend upon fallen leaves for survival. Over winter months, many species of butterflies or moths exist as pupa or caterpillars in leaf litter, and if these leaves are removed, entire insect populations are destroyed. Without insects in the leaf litter, birds that might have come to the yard looking for food for their young will go elsewhere. Any excess of leaves, if some special neatness is required, should be placed in the compost pit and returned to the soil after they have decomposed.

THE EXECUTION OF THE DESIGN

At this juncture, it will be presumed that the homeowner has produced a sylvan landscape design, is in possession of a suburban home, and is of right mind and sound will. Financially, there is nothing that requires the design to be executed all at once, as it can be done in stages, in parcels, or in any convenient manner.

Municipal Codes and Credits

Before breaking ground, it is wise to expose the sylvan design to the local municipal fathers and seek their blessing. Given the change in today's climate, city managers should be all too happy to encourage their fellow citizens to plant native trees, to irrigate less, and to stop dumping pesticides into the communal groundwater. The best approach to these managers is with a completed bubble diagram in hand, one that has a clear listing of native plants, and that will ensure that the amount of runoff water decreases while its purity increases. Hopefully, a sylvan landscape, with whatever height of ground cover the homeowner desires to take root, will bring a tear of joy to the staid municipal eye.

Many states and cities offer tax credits or other incentives for similar projects, not only for homeowners who plant new trees but also to those who will replace their turf grass with some more humane ground cover. Some examples:

- Houston requires those desirous of obtaining incentives to produce a type of plan now familiar to the reader: "A landscape plan is a drawing that identifies the locations of existing and proposed utility lines, roadways, sidewalks, streetlights, trees, shrubs, ground covers, natural features, landscape buffers, other landscape elements, and planting or construction details. Make certain that the plant species and planting size of all trees and shrubs are noted on the plan. All protected trees on the plan must be identified for preservation, transplanting, or removal. Applicants must submit a landscape plan for review when applying for a development plan or building permit."

- The state of Minnesota has set aside $900,000 to assist homeowners in replacing turf grass with pollinator-friendly ground cover, assistance that could cover up to 75% of the cost of conversion.[*]

- Olympia, Washington, requires homeowners to maintain a minimum number of trees per square foot, measured in tree units that are directly proportional to the tree's diameter; the larger the tree's girth, the more units. There are incentives for attaining an above-average number of tree units. Olympia's forest plan is to build a continuous network of urban forests that connect streets, squares, and parks to regional greenbelts, forests, and agricultural lands. Olympia's urban forestry goal is more poetic than most: "Trees of various species, ages, and sizes are growing in all parts of the city, contributing to a green and healthy community. Tall slender conifers accentuate and add beauty to the skyline. Graceful tree branches arch over busy thoroughfares and quiet residential streets. Wooded corridors weave through the city, providing for the coexistence of wildlife habitat, play areas for children, and recreational space for all citizens . . . . Evergreen trees grow throughout the city, a visual reminder of the special character of the Pacific Northwest. Deciduous trees mark the seasons, connecting us visually with the passage of time. Shady areas in public places welcome citizens on a summer's day and provide shelter from the rain."

Search for a Partner

During the design process, it was suggested that the homeowner identify and use the online resources of local PN&Ls (plant nursery/landscaping) to research the availability of native plants and determine their respective costs. If this research was not done then, it should be done now. Contact these PN&Ls—in person, via email, or both—to show them the design and any supporting notes made concerning the sizes of plants at purchase, details and materials for hardscape, soil replacement, grading, and other elements. Hear what the PN&Ls have to say or suggest. The feedback from these initial encounters will provide an excellent opportunity to modify or clarify certain elements of the design. It may also be possible to get a feel for the time required to install the new landscape. When enough information has been gathered, choose the PN&Ls that inspire the most confidence and ask for references.

When you are satisfied with a PN&Ls references, ask for a written quote for the execution of the design. Ask that the quote is specific as to: (a) the amount of time that it will take to complete the project, (b) the availability and price of all plants, (c) the details of any work the PN&L intends to subcontract, and (d) what plant guarantees are offered. Note: plant guarantees are always tied to a required degree of maintenance. While post-guarantee yearly maintenance of the landscape may not be a part of the PN&Ls quote, this is still the moment to ask for an estimate. Review all

---

[*] This bill, introduced by Representative Kelly Morrison, was approved by the legislature.

quotes carefully. After completing the review, the homeowner is equipped to make sound judgments on who to proceed with and how to proceed.

In the course of negotiating for the final costs of the execution of the design, any last errors may be revealed and hopefully corrected before it comes to contracting for goods and services. Moreover, if some plants are unavailable, or if work cannot be completed as originally planned, a remedy will be found, sometimes more realistic. This way, when the earth is finally opened and the work begins, the homeowner will have a degree of certainty about when the work will end.

FUTURE VISIONS

Trees live for centuries but, unlike their owners, never move. The life span of any house depends more upon external factors than the solidity of its construction. But the laws of probability, so true in general, so fallacious in particular, should still allow for young trees the time to mature. If the homeowner has completed the exercise in the preceding chapter and applied these lessons to their own design, they will have a reasonable vision of what the future landscape holds.

Gaining a precise idea of what a landscape, designed today, will look like in the future requires the art of divination—an innate gift rather than an art that could be learned. Augury,[*] the art of predicting the future by interpreting the flights of birds, would also seem to be an innate gift. Lacking the gift of divination and the skill of landscape painting, the following few illustrations, drawn from my plant choices in the first two exercises in the chapter precedent, are but poor reflections of the sylvan landscapes I imagine. Excuses made, I offer a few of my visions:

View A of Exercise #1, 5th year after planting, in October

The flowering dogwood toward the back right is now 8 years old, about 10 feet high, and in flower. The dogwoods have all been pruned to favor a system of low-spreading branches that do not overlap and that will lead to vase-shaped crowns. The eastern redbuds in the forefront and to the left are now 8 years old, around 10 feet in height, and have all been pruned to give them a close-to-the-ground, multitrunk shape.

As the house (shown in profile) is considered to have been slightly raised on its foundation, the heights of the shrub-rows have been staggered, lower by the sidewalk and higher by the house, giving the terrain an impression of relief when viewed from the sidewalk. Over the past 5 years, the different species of shrubs in the shrub-rows have intermingled. To the left, the black chokeberry and mountain laurel shrub-rows have come together, although the latter will not bloom until June. The Virginia roses in the shrub-row on the right are in bloom.

The partridgeberry's evergreen, ovate, shiny leaves have covered all the empty ground in the front yard and have made inroads into the disintegrating mulch at the base of the trees. Its small white flowers will continue to bloom through summer, when they will be accompanied by bright red, attractive berries.

---

[*]   From the Latin *auspicium* and *auspex*, meaning "one who looks at birds." Depending upon the bird's species or the direction of its flight, a specific portion of the future would be revealed.

Hartford in October
View A

Hartford in May
View A

View A of Exercise #1, 10th year after planting, in May (previous page)

The flowering dogwood toward the back left is now 13 years old, about 15 feet high, and with red leaves. The eastern redbuds in the forefront are also 15 years old, they have attained their full height of 12 feet, and their leaves have turned yellow-gold. To the left, the black chokeberry has lost most of its leaves and a Baltimore oriole is finishing off the last of its berries. The mountain laurel, entwined with its evergreen companion, now bears fruit. The Virginia rose in the shrub-row on the right still has a few green leaves. The partridgeberry's evergreen, shiny leaves have replaced all the mulch, and its red berries are ripe.

View B of Exercise #1, 10th year after planting, in October (below)

The common persimmon in the forefront, now 13 years old and 18 feet tall, has been pruned to favor the stronger branches that will carry its rather heavy fruit. The fruits are now ripe and should be picked after the first frost, when the cold weather has increased their sugar content. The fast-growing red maple in the back right is now 13 years old and over 20 feet in height. Its lower branches have spread out naturally, starting at about 10 feet from the ground, while its upper branches reach upward. The slow-growing mountain maple in the back left, now 12 feet tall, has been pruned to become a large, low-growing shrub that will shield the paved space from the neighbors.

Hartford in October
View B

The black chokeberry, Virginia rose, and evergreen inkberry, from the shrub-row in the foreground, are now bearing fruits or berries, and the deciduous amongst them have taken on their fall colors. The highbush blueberry to the right, kept to an easy picking height of about 5 feet, has finished fruiting and its excellent fall color is a mix of red, yellow, orange, and purple. The shrub-row under the red maple tree, composed of the shade-tolerant mountain laurel, American hazelnut, and arrowwood, has come into its own.

The evergreen partridgeberry in the foreground now has red berries to contrast with its dark green leaves. The mulch path, which has now been refreshed a few times, has made peace with the partridgeberry and surrounds the trunk of the persimmon tree toward the back. The wild ginger has colonized all its allotted space, has a tendency to be evergreen, and could easily advance and encroach upon or intermingle with the partridgeberry.

View A of Exercise #2, 10th year after planting, in June (below)

The American hornbeam in the forefront, now 16 feet tall, has fleshed out, and its crown has been pruned to remain close to the ground. When this hornbeam approaches its height of 20 to 25 feet, its trunk will thicken and its fluted blue-gray bark will provide additional interest in winter. The downy serviceberry in the background, also 16 feet tall, has shed its flowers and its Saskatoon berries will soon be

Atlanta in June

ripe for the picking and putting into pies and jellies. On the far right, the American yellow-wood is in full flower.

To look through the pergola is to look at the American wisteria, now in full bloom. As the wisteria's flowers only grow on new wood, care-ful pruning can greatly increase the number of racemes. The red buckeyes at the back are a full 10 feet high and have been pruned to be a large multi-trunked hedge rather than a small tree. The buckeyes now shelter and frame the wild-flower garden.

Just behind the heartleaf foamflowers in the foreground, the Pennsylvania sedge, under the trees and bordering the low retaining wall, has been kept cut where foot traffic could approach the pergola. The rows of clasping and white milkweeds, fronting the buckeyes, are now in bloom and should prove irresistible to migrat-ing monarch butterflies. The blooms will last much of the summer.

———

Rather than continue to infuse the reader with visions reminiscent of vegetable soup, I will stop here.

CHAPTER 10

"John the Revelator"

Well who's that a writing? John the Revelator
Who's that a writing, John the Revelator
Who's that a writing, John the Revelator
A book of the Seven Seals.
Tell me what's John a writing? Ask the Revelator
What's John a writing? Ask the Revelator
What's John a writing? Ask the Revelator
A book of the Seven Seals
Now who art worthy, thousands cried holy
Bound for some, Son of our God,
Daughter of Zion, Judah the Lion
He redeemeth, and bought us with His blood
Well what's John a writing? Ask the Revelator
Who's that a writing, John the Revelator
Who's that a writing, John the Revelator
A book of the Seven Seals
—"John the Revelator," Blind Willie Johnson

IN SUB-SAHARAN African cultures, call and response is a common pattern of participation in religious rituals as well as in musical expression. The pattern consists of a succession of two distinct phrases, where the second phrase is heard as a direct commentary on or in response to the first. Enslaved Africans carried this form of music with them after they were captured and ferried to the New World. Once Christianized, call and response appeared in the slaves' versions of gospel songs, and during the protracted period of their emancipation, this same musical form found its way into the blues.

Blind Willie Johnson, an itinerant street preacher and singer, certainly understood these gospel facts when he composed and sang "John the Revelator," as did Willie B. Harris, his common-law wife who accompanied him. Blind Willie's rough voice and his violent mastery of the slide guitar pose the questions of the damned, while Willie Harris responds with the hopeful voice of the saved. Their call-and-response vocals convey a sense of impending doom with the possibility of salvation that finds an echo in the environment's struggle for salvation in an industrial world.

APOCALYPSE NOW

The concept of an apocalypse derives from an ancient Greek word meaning "revelation" or the "heralding of events previously not known." While the term apocalypse once implied the advent of a sinister event of a religious cast, its usage has been extended to mean the end of something. The three kinds of generally accepted apocalypses, described below in ascending order of probability, are the spiritual, the natural, and the human-made.

- Spiritual apocalypses, prophet-driven for the most part, involve the removal of the totality of the human species, those waiting in purgatory and those alive on earth, with a general exception for the wildlife.

On the bright side, spiritual apocalypses have a 0% chance of occurrence. Although never witnessed, these shakedowns from on high have been remarkably well described. For example, Revelation (of John), the last book of the New Testament, is fraught with harrowing detail about what trumpets will sound, what seals will be broken, and what signs will herald the End of Days. Yet, the first six of the seven trumpet blasts are usually interpreted to be wake-up calls, a time for the wicked to repent, a time for the righteous to rejoice.

- Natural apocalypses, such as the earth colliding with Manhattan-sized meteorites, massive eruptions of chains of volcanoes, or tsunamis the heights of large buildings, have less than a 0.0001% chance of happening during any one person's lifetime, but happen they will. The geological record is chock-a-block with world-shattering events that have destroyed whatever life lay in their path. Nor would advance knowledge of the date of arrival of a natural apocalypse make the event any more palatable for those whose inevitable fate it is to be consumed.

- Human-made apocalypses, the end product of the Anthropocene, have proven to be 99% predictable, doggedly unavoidable, and strangely self-heralding. Ecological collapse and disastrous climate change now top the list of imminent apocalypses. Without delving too deeply into the possible timing of either, both could arrive before this century ends unless humankind behaves differently.

The present harbingers of ecological collapse are all too familiar. We continually hear about insect, bee, frog, bird, animal, and fish apocalypses. There is a fast-growing list of species lined up and ready to join their stuffed cousins in museums with the word "extinct" engraved in brass just under their scientific name. If you care about the planet and the people and animals that live on it, there are two ways to go: you can feel ever more frustrated by the world's inaction, or you can rethink what you can do to improve the world's lot.

There are few secular or religious texts that give hope to apocalyptic misgivings, yet hope is available to those who are uniquely able to contribute, as all property owners have the means to battle, albeit on a modest scale, ecological collapse and climate change. This is not to lay the fate of the natural world squarely upon turf-grass enthusiasts, but perhaps it is time for the suburbs to give back. And to raise a call to action. The signs trumpeting the destruction of the world's ecosystems have sounded, and everyone has heard, seen, or felt them. The only remaining question is who will heed the call? There is strength in numbers, and perhaps it is the happy fate of the estimated 174 million American suburbanites to be able to accomplish more where others have failed.

Willie B. Harris responded to the call on a hopeful note, and so shall I. My faith is in the suburbs.

APPENDIX
NORTH AMERICAN PLANT VIGNETTES

"Native plants give us a sense of where we are in this great land of ours. I want Texas to look like Texas and Vermont to look like Vermont."
—Lady Bird Johnson

NATIVE PLANT intermediaries, such as landscape architects, plant nurseries, and social media gardening platforms, facilitate native plant selections that would otherwise fall to the lot of the homeowner. Like matchmakers in the marriage market, plant intermediaries assist with or execute one or more of three market functions:

1. Searching, i.e. the gathering of information relevant to the transaction;

2. Matching, i.e. bringing parties compatible as transaction partners; and

3. Transaction, i.e. the negotiation of the transaction and finalizing the transaction agreement.

By preforming these functions, market intermediaries reduce search costs, increase matching quality, and advance the connection process. For both planting and mating, the intermediary acquires information about the eligible, determines which make a good match, and facilitates the process of interaction. The consent of the bride and groom was of little or no importance to matrimonial matchmakers, and plant intermediaries often have fixed ideas of what is right. However, for both humans and plants, the ability to grow and thrive together weighs far more heavily upon the chosen than upon the choosers.

But what about love? Jane Austen, in almost all her novels but particularly *Pride and Prejudice*, clearly believed that one should only marry for love and heaps biting scorn and satire on the matchmakers. Alas, this adamant chronicler of true love never seemed to have found hers. When it comes to plants, those who have tried and failed, myself included, to grow an avocado tree using its pit, four toothpicks, and a wide-mouthed bottle of water, know full well that love cannot replace favorable husbandry, proper climate, and fertile soil.

So what was I to do when choosing the regional native plants for my imagined landscaping designs, knowing full well that the niceties of matchmaking and husbandry, as well as the infinite variations of climate and soil, where beyond my grasp? My solution, as evidenced by the following vignettes, was to follow the advice of the dean of Roman writers, Marcus Tullus Cicero, who opined that, "If you have a garden and a library, you have everything you need."* This because the Roman garden was designed

---

* Letter to Varro, 46 BCE

for thinking, philosophizing, and discourse; it was a garden library, rather than a library with a garden. In light of the political and moral implications of Roman gardening, I have opted to select those regional native plants, with a few poignant exceptions, whose history, folklore, and medicinal qualities (real or imaginary) caught my fancy. I would dote my imaginary suburban yards with trappings of literacy, food for thought and wildlife, and a nod to the culinary and the apothecary, while trying to limit my botanical observations to a single introductory sentence.

This is not to say that my landscape designs in Chapter 9 are not serious, they are very much so, as it requires a method to introduce so many trees and shrubs into a confined space subject to suburban strictures. To illustrate both my serious landscape designs and my rather frivolous choice of native plants, I attach an easily deciphered schematic of the six exercises precedent, as well as the character sketches of the chosen plants, all in the hope that the former can serve as a model for the homeowner and the latter as inspiration.

EXERCISE #1: PLANTS NATIVE TO THE NORTHEAST

Trees

BASSWOOD—*TILIA AMERICANA* (X#1-N°1):
A medium- to plus-sized deciduous tree with a moderate growth rate that can attain a 20-year height of 25 feet. Also known as a linden or a bee tree, the basswood has a long history of use by both American Indians and their invasive cousins, the Europeans. The medieval Teutonic tribes associated basswood with judgment and truth and their judges returned verdicts *Unter der Linden*. The French brew an infusion from linden blossoms called *tilleul* and attempt to

cure their nervous irritability by taking hot baths flavored with these flowers. The basswood's flowers provide abundant nectar for bees, and smaller mammals relish its seeds.

SHAGBARK HICKORY—*CARYA OVEA* (X#1-N°2):
A large deciduous tree with a slow growth rate that can attain a 20-year height of 20 feet. The shagbark hickory is in the same phylum as pecans and walnuts. The problem for humans, not squirrels, is how to get at the nutmeat, as the shells are incredibly hard. American Indians smashed the entire nut, boiled them in water, then filtered out the particulates, leaving the hickory milk called *pawcohiccora*, shortened by the colonialists to *pohichery*, believed to have led to the name *hickory*. Hickory nuts are the chocolate-chip cookies of the squirrel world.

RED MAPLE—*ACER RUBRUM* (X#1-N°3):
A medium-sized deciduous tree with a fast growth rate that can attain a 20-year height of 30 feet. The red maple has an Asian counterpart that was described by a Chinese sage as: "Bestowing perfume for the nose, color for the eye, and sweetness for the tongue." The fortune cookie left out the delights of its whirly winged seeds that are useful to wildlife after the forest's tastier items have disappeared. The red maple's winged seeds are sticky when opened and are often used by small children to decorate their noses. We do not know, but seriously doubt, if American Indians ever made maple syrup before the arrival of the Europeans.

CHERRY BIRCH—*BETULA LENTA* (X#1-N°4): A medium- to minus-sized deciduous tree with a moderate growth rate that can attain a 20-year height of 20 feet. The cherry birch was once a source of birch beer and oil of wintergreen, both of which have mercifully failed to maintain their popularity in the 21st century. Another tradition that has fallen out of favor is whipping miscreants with birch boughs. First popularized by the Britons who used birch boughs, rather than the cudgel, to flog miscreants because "birchen twigs break no ribs," a tradition embraced by the colonial settlers and only abandoned in the 1950s. Thomas Jefferson, America's third president and amorous slaveholder, enacted laws that provided up to 15 birchen lashes for individuals pretending to practice witchcraft.

COMMON PERSIMMON—*DIOSPYROS VIRGINIANA* (X#1-N°5): A medium- to minus-sized deciduous tree with a slow growth rate that can attain a 20-year height of 15 feet. The common persimmon is a member of the ebony family and, like ebony, its heartwood is almost black. The persimmon's edible fruits are incredibly bitter until ripe, and then somewhat bitter when ripe, but are rather tasty in jellies. Occasionally, an up-and-coming chef will try to sneak an unadulterated persimmon into a desert but never with great success. A study has suggested that the persimmon fruit is an evolutionary remnant once consumed by the megafauna that roamed the North American continent 10,000 years ago, and that mammoths would have been better at consuming the fruit and dispersing its seeds than today's squirrels.[*]

AMERICAN HOLLY—*ILEX OPACA* (X#1-N°6): A medium- to minus-sized evergreen tree with a slow growth rate that can attain a 20-year height of 15 feet. Thanks to the American holly's thorns, that inculcate suffering, its berries, that evoke drops of blood, and its leaves, that resemble the flames of hell, it has been inextricably bound to Christianity and Christmas. Less given to superstition, American Indians used the dried berries as decorative buttons.

Whether or not the holly's symbolism has rendered its fruit extremely toxic to humans may yet be a subject of pagan debate, but they are an important late winter survival food for birds, once other food sources have been exhausted.

MOUNTAIN MAPLE—*ACER SPICATEM* (X#1-N°7): A small deciduous tree with a moderate growth rate that can be pruned to remain at heights of around 12 feet. The mountain maple is the preferred winter food of the white-tailed deer, not that luring deer into the suburban yard is a particularly useful idea, but if deer must come to the suburban yard, best they come in winter. François Michaux,[**] the famed 19th-century French botanist, needlessly maligned the lovely mountain maple when he wrote: "It is found in the gardens of the curious, rather to complete the series of species, than for any remarkable property of its foliage or flowers."

RED MULBERRY—*MORUS RUBRA* (X#1-N°8): A small to plus-sized deciduous tree with a fast growth rate that can attain a 20-year height of 20 feet. The red mulberry's European cousins have inspired artists, notably Vincent van Gogh, a few chefs, regrettably not Escoffier, and a children's song, "Here we go, round the mulberry bush." Rather than paint or sing about the red mulberry, the ingredients for a 9-inch pie are as follows: for the filling, three cups of mulberries and one and a quarter cups of sugar; and for the crust, a quarter-cup of flour, two and a half teaspoons of butter, and one tablespoon of milk. As the red mulberry's fruits ripen early and are devoured by birds, best to make these delicious pies quickly.

FLOWERING DOGWOOD—*CORNUS FLORIDA* (X#1-N°9): A small to plus-sized deciduous tree with a slow growth rate that can be pruned to remain at a height of 15 feet. The flowering dog-

[*]   *Southeastern Naturalist*, 14: 22–32
[**]   *The North American Sylva* (1811), François Michaux

wood's flowers are not flowers at all but specialized leaves called *bracts*. After the Victorians had ascribed a sentimental meaning to the dogwood's flowers, local divines went further and promulgated the story that the wood of the dogwood tree was used to construct the true cross. A fable easily disproven, given that the dogwood is not native to the Middle East or Europe. Also, as many European churches claim to have a fragment of the true cross, carbon dating shows these fragments to be from the 11th century, and not one of them was dogwood. Similar clouds of doubt swirl about the Holy Nails.

EASTERN REDBUD—*CERCIS CANADAENIS* (X#1-N°10): A small to plus-sized deciduous tree with a fast growth rate that can be pruned to remain at a height of around 15 feet. The eastern redbud is also called a Judas tree because, it is said, Judas Iscariot, after having betrayed Jesus, hung himself on a hopefully taller specimen. In that redbuds are common to Judea, a more secular idea is that Judea's tree had its name shortened to Judas tree. The blossoms of the eastern redbud look very similar to peas; the tree belongs to the same legume plant family. Like peas, the eastern redwood's blossoms are edible and can add a bright citrusy taste to salads.

GINGKO—*GINGKO BILBOA* (X#1-N°11): A non-native medium- to minus-sized deciduous tree with a slow growth rate that can attain a 20-year height of 16 feet. The gingko, once native everywhere, would now not seem to be native anywhere. Being the only living species left of its phyla, the gingko's origins are uncertain; their cultivation seems to have predated their genesis. Gingkoes would probably be extinct today were they not cultivated in antiquity by Chinese Buddhist monks, who continue to debate whether or not there were ever any native trees. As a matter of conservation con-

cern, planting a gingko will help preserve the remnants of this living fossil.

Shrubs

HIGHBUSH BLUEBERRY—*VACCINIUM CORYMBOSUM* (X#1-N°12): A medium- to plus-sized deciduous shrub with a moderate growth rate that is best trimmed to a height that favors berry-picking children. After the fruit of the highbush blueberry became fashionable amongst dietetic gurus, this humble but tasty berry was imbued with qualities that were reputed to improve memory, retard aging, prevent certain types of cancer, and spread everlasting joy. Despite or perhaps because of these attributes, blueberries make for great snacks and excellent muffins.

SOUTHERN ARROWWOOD—*VIBURNAM DENTATE* (X#1-N°13): A medium-sized deciduous shrub with a moderate growth rate that is best trimmed to a height of between 4 and 6 feet. American Indians used the southern arrowwood's straight stems to fabricate arrow shafts, hence its name. They also made a poultice from the plant that reduced any swelling of the legs experienced by a woman after she has given birth, hence its usefulness in a more fashion-conscious age. The southern arrowwood provides food, cover, and nesting sites for birds, as well as larval food for butterflies and moths.

AMERICAN HAZELNUT—*CORYLUS AMERICANA* (X#1-N°14): A medium deciduous shrub with a moderate growth rate that is best trimmed to a height of between 4 and 8 feet. The American hazelnut's illustrious European cousins are cherished by The Order of Bards, Ovates and Druids, a fashionable druidic order headquartered in England. These neo-druids say: "The hazel might be said to be the quintessential Celtic tree because of its legendary position at the ear of the Otherworld. Here, nine magic hazel-trees hand over the Well of Wisdom." For similar occult reasons, druids use hazelwood to make magic wands. On both sides of the Atlantic, for druids and scoffers alike, the hazelnut will bear an annual crop of delicious edible nuts that drop free of the husk when mature and are easy to crack open.

BLACK CHOKEBERRY—*ARONIA MELANP-CARPA* (X#1-N°15): A medium-sized deciduous shrub with a moderate growth rate that is best trimmed to a height of between 4 and 6 feet. Despite its unappealing name, the black chokeberry's berries will not cause choking, but they will make you pucker up if eaten raw, something the American Indians declined to do. Some consider the raw seeds poisonous, while others rave about the fruits' health benefits. Jelly is a safe bet.

MAPLE-LEAF VIBURNUM—*VIBURNUM ACER-IFOLIUM* (X#1-N°16): A medium-sized deciduous shrub with a moderate growth rate that is best trimmed to a height between 4 and 6 feet. Solely within the guarded realms of naturopathic medicine and shamanism, a poultice made from the chewed, unopened flower buds of the maple-leaf viburnum, generously applied to lip sores, is reputed to have both a healing and a soothing effect. These same occult sources consider that an infusion of the crushed inner bark is a cure for dysentery. The more practical pollinators, such as butterflies and bees, are partial to the flowers while the birds gobble up the berries.

VIRGINIA ROSE—*ROSA VIRGINIA* (X#1-N°17): A medium-sized deciduous shrub with a moderate growth rate that is best trimmed to a height of between 4 to 6 feet. The Virginia rose, like many other roses, is a symbolic carrier of secrets. The term "sub rosa" comes from the Roman tradition of hanging roses over meeting places with the understanding that anything said "under the rose" will never be repeated. The flowers have special value to native bees, and their fruits, known as hips, can be used to make teas and jellies.

COMMON BUTTONBUSH—*CAPHALANTHUS OCCIDENTALIS* (X#1-N°18): A medium-sized deciduous shrub with a moderate growth rate that is best trimmed to a height of between 4 and 6 feet. The common buttonbush does not serve its namesake adequately; the image is amiss, given that a button is a flattened disk. Its local name of honey-ball is a far more appropriate moniker; both hummingbirds and bees are attracted by the abundance of nectar found in its aromatic flower balls.

EVERGREEN INKBERRY—*ILEX GLABDA* (X#1-N°19): A medium-sized evergreen shrub with a slow growth rate that is best trimmed to a height of between 4 and 6 feet. Locally called gallberry, the black drupes of the evergreen inkberry, unlike the fruit of many other hollies, are hardly a cause for yuletide celebration as they grow under the leaves and remain obscure from an ornamental point of view. Its leaves, when dried and roasted, were reputedly used by American Indians to brew a black tea-like drink, remembered today as Appalachian tea. The flowers bloom at the beginning of May and last for almost a month, during which time they literally drip with nectar and are the source of the highly prized gallberry honey.

MOUNTAIN LAUREL—*KALMIA LATIFOLIA* (X#1-N°20): A medium-sized evergreen shrub with a moderate growth rate that is best trimmed to a height of between 4 and 6 feet. The mountain laurel, besides being the Connecticut state flower, is notable for its unusual method of

to remain at heights of 15 feet or less. The downy serviceberry's edible berries, known as Saskatoon berries in the Canadian providence of Manitoba, are what have made Saskatoon pie famous with our northern neighbors. The berries of the downy serviceberry are slightly larger than blueberries, possibly more nutritious, and can be prepared in all the same delicious ways.

MAYHAW—*CRATAEGUS AESTIVALIS* (X#2-N°7): A small deciduous tree with a moderate growth rate that can be pruned to remain at heights of 15 feet or less. A member of the hawthorn family, the mayhaw's berries are tart and tasteless when raw but sweet and delicious when they ripen in May, hence the tree's name. The berries will fall to the ground if the tree is shaken, allowing the berry-pickers to avoid the tree's thorns and gather the berries easily to make the finest jelly the South has to offer. Best be quick; the wildlife, starved for fruit over winter, will pounce upon the berries as soon as they are ripe.

WASHINGTON HAWTHORN—*CRATAEGUS PHAENOPYRUM* (X#2-N°8): A medium-sized deciduous tree with a fast growth rate that can attain a 20-year height of 20 feet. The Washington Hawthorn's showy white flowers are beautiful, and their berries are delicious. The berry's seeds, however, are said to be poisonous. Therefore, for the daring, eat the berries and spit out the seeds. The hawthorn has added dangers for berry-pickers: its branches have sharp thorns.

Shrubs

RED BUCKEYE—*AESCULUS PAVIA* (X#2-N°9): A large deciduous shrub with a fast growth rate that is best trimmed to a height between 7 and 10 feet. The red buckeye's scarlet tubular flowers are oft pollinated by the ruby-throated hummingbird, and their seeds, which have the appearance of a deer's eye (hence the shrub's name), while toxic to humans, are gobbled up by the wildlife.

AMERICAN BEAUTYBERRY—*CALLICARPA AMERICANA* (X#2-N°10): A medium-sized deciduous shrub with a moderate growth rate that is best trimmed to a height between 4 and 6 feet. As a folk remedy, the crushed leaves of the American beautyberry were said to repel biting insects, a theory since borne out by studies at the University of Mississippi, whose professors, living deep in the heart of mosquito country, are sure to know about such things.

SWEETSHRUB—*CALYCANTHUS FLORIDUS* (X#2-N°11): A medium-sized deciduous shrub with a moderate growth rate that is best kept trimmed to a height of 4 to 6 feet. Calycanthus oil, distilled from the sweetshrub's delicately scented flowers, is used as an essential oil in high-quality perfumes. There are stories that its bark was once used as a substitute for cinnamon, hence its local name, Carolina allspice. That the sweetshrub smells so good is reason enough to plant it near a door or patio.

STRAWBERRY BUSH—*EUONYMUS GARDENIA* (X#2-N°12): A medium- to minus-sized deciduous shrub with a moderate growth rate that is best trimmed to a height between 3 and 5 feet. The strawberry bush is commonly called heart-a-bustin' to better describe the colorful, heart-shaped fruit that appears to be exploding from its capsule. The strawberry bush's seeds are reputed to be a particularly effective laxative.

DWARF FOTHERGILLA—*FOTHERGILLA GARDENIA* (X#2-N°13): A very small deciduous shrub with a slow growth rate that is hopefully raised to a height of 3 feet. The dwarf fothergilla is a size-impaired shrub that is a welcome addition to the liberally inclined shrub-row that welcomes diversity and encourages the unique. The dwarf fothergilla's lovely flowers also welcome, without discrimination, the butterfly, the bee, and the hummingbird.

OAKLEAF HYDRANGEA—*HYDRANGEA QUADRIFOLIA* (X#2-N°14): A medium-sized deciduous shrub with a moderate growth rate that is best trimmed to a height between 4 and 6 feet. Hydrangeas, albeit popular everywhere, are mostly of Asiatic origin. Only two species, of which the oakleaf hydrangea is one, are native to the United States and only in its southeastern quadrant. The oakleaf hydrangea has the distinction of being the only member of its genus that can provide color and beauty in all four seasons; its leaves stay on the plant and keep their fall colors throughout winter.

WINTERBERRY—*ILEX VERTICILLATA* (X#2-N°15): A medium-sized deciduous shrub with a slow growth rate that is best kept trimmed to a height between 4 and 6 feet. The winterberry, as its name suggests, provides an excellent food source for wildlife during winter and early spring. Both the robin and the bluebird are particularly fond of its berries. Because only fertilized female winterberry shrubs will produce berries, it is critical that there be at least one pollinating male nearby.

DROOPING LEUCOTHOE—*LEUCOTHOE FONTANESIANA* (X#2-N°16): A medium-sized evergreen shrub with a slow growth rate that is best trimmed to a height between 4 and 6 feet. The drooping leucothoe, locally known as doghobble, has branches than droop from the fatigue of holding up its pendulous clusters of white flowers. Weighted down, these branches reach the soil and take root at their tips, creating an extensive impenetrable tangle. It is said that a bear, fleeing a hunter's dogs, will head into a tangle of drooping leucothoe to hobble the dog's feet.

Vines, Ground Cover, and Wildflowers

AMERICAN WISTERIA—*WISTERIA FRUTESCENS* (X#2-N°17): A high-climbing deciduous vine that can attain a length of 50 feet. The American wisteria, contrary to its Asian counterparts, twines clockwise and has smaller unscented flowers (racemes). Wisterias are long-lived powerful vines that need strong support, metal often being more reliable than wood.

HEARTLEAF FOAMFLOWER—*TIARELLE CORDIFOLIA* (X#2-N°18): A perennial flowering herb that spreads by underground stems, thrives in shade, and grows to a height of 1 to 2 feet. The heartleaf foamflower's scientific name, *Tiarelle,* comes from the diminutive of the Greek word *tiara*, meaning crown, and refers to the flower's shape. Its leaves have a high tannin content making them a natural astringent.

GREEN-AND-GOLD—*CHRYSOGONUM VIRGINIANUM* (X#2-N°19): A creeping, perennial semi-evergreen herb that grows to a height of 6 to 10 inches. The green-and-gold, often called golden knee, bears clusters of yellow flowers that give rise to its scientific name, *Chrysogonum*, derived from the Greek word for gold ("chryos") and for knee ("gonum"), because its gold-colored flowers originate at the leaf's axis.

PENNSYLVANIA SEDGE—*CAREX PENSYLVAVICA* (X#2-N°20): A semi-evergreen, shade tolerant, low-growing perennial leaf that spreads by rhizomes and grows to a height of 10 to 16 inches. If mowing proves to be an incurable habit or a recurring desire, Pennsylvania sedge, once established, can be mowed three or four times a year and turned into a beautiful lawn, albeit one that will not tolerate much foot traffic.

DWARF SMILAX—*SMILAX PUMILLA* (X#2-N°21): A broadleaf, ground-hugging, evergreen vine with a slow growth rate that can grow to a height of 5 to 8 inches. The dwarf smilax is also called the sarsaparilla vine as its roots were used to flavor root beer and other beverages. Its berries are said to be edible and even delicious. Wildlife readily consumes all parts of the dwarf smilax, from its roots to its berries.

Wildflowers

CLASPING MILKWEED—*ASCLEPIAS AMPLEX-ICAULIS* (X#2-N°22): A stout, glabrous (without hairs), perennial wildflower that grows to a height of 2 to 3 feet. The clasping milkweed bears pink to purplish flowers that clasp to the stem and has special value to bumblebees as well as monarch butterflies.

WHITE MILKWEED—*ASCLEPIAS VARIGATA* (X#2-N°23): An herbaceous, perennial wildflower that grows to a height of 2 to 3 feet. The white milkweed's large showy flowers are white except for a narrow purple ring between the petals and the hooded corona, a source of its other common name, red-ring milkweed.

GEORGIA WILDFLOWER MIX (X#2-N°24): The State Botanical Garden of Georgia has developed a Georgia wildflower seed mix with native pollinators in mind. After years of research, they finally have enough extra seeds to sell to the public.

EXERCISE #3: PLANTS NATIVE TO THE MIDWEST

Trees

SHORTLEAF PINE—*PINUS ECHINATA* (X#3-N°1): A medium- to plus-sized evergreen tree with a fast growth rate that can attain a 20-year height of 20 feet. The shortleaf pine, Missouri's only native pine species, was once far more widespread than it is today. The shortleaf pine, a true pioneer species, evolved in a landscape that had a historic mean fire interval of 2 to 20 years, from both natural and human sources. When, at the beginning of the 20th century, a policy of fire suppression began, the few shortleaf pines that had survived the harrow of the lumber industry declined even further. Today, the remaining shortleaf pine trees are mostly found in the protected areas of the Ozarks. Conservationists now promote replanting shortleaf pines, not only for their intrinsic value but also for the sake of the plants and animals associated with them.

RIVER BIRCH—*BETULA NIGRA* (X#3-N°2): A medium-sized deciduous tree with a fast growth rate, which can be pruned to have multiple trunks and to maintain a height of 15 feet. Naturally occurring only in the floodplain of the Mississippi River in eastern Missouri, the river birch is prized for its incredible peeling bark. The bark is salmon-pink, smooth and shiny at first, but later when the tree ages, the bark flakes and curls in cinnamon-brown to blackish sheets.

PECAN—*CARYA ILLINOINSIS* (X#3-N°3): A medium- to plus-sized deciduous tree with a moderate-plus growth rate that can attain a 20-year height of 25 feet. Pecan trees have both male and female flowers that do not bloom at the same time, resulting in a tree that cannot self-cross-pollinate and produce nuts. So, if there is not another pecan tree in the vicinity, be sure to plant two. Although wild pecans were well known among native and colonial Americans, the trees were not domesticated, hence not well known outside their native range. Once domesticated, pecan nuts became increasingly popular for their rich, buttery flavor, either when eaten fresh or used in cooking.

SUGARBERRY—*CELYIS LAEVIGATA* (X#3-N°4): A medium- to plus-sized deciduous tree with a moderate growth rate that can attain a 20-year height of 20 feet. The fruit of the aptly named sugarberry is indeed sweet, edible, and particularly attractive to a large variety of Missouri's wildlife, albeit birds have the edge over all others. When ripe, the sugarberry's fruits, taste is similar to dates, except the stone is large and covered only by a thin layer of flesh. The sugarberry tree does not produce fruits until it is nearly full grown, and then its fruits are maddeningly out of the reach of humans. American Indians were said to have been quite fond of the sugarberry despite the inordinate amount of work and danger it takes to harvest a handful or two before the birds get them all. The war-like Comanche, little remembered for their culinary skills, beat the fruits to a pulp, mixed the pulp with animal fat, rolled the mixture into balls, and roasted them in the fire.

KENTUCKY COFFEETREE—*GYMNOCLADUS DIOICUS* (X#3-N°5): A medium-sized deciduous tree with a moderate to fast growth rate that can attain a 20-year height of 20 feet. The Kentucky coffeetree's late-emerging and early falling leaves can result in the tree being bare for up to 6 months. This, and the fact that its large leaves mean but few twigs in the winter profile, makes it the ideal tree for cooler urban settings where winter sunlight needs to be maximized. It is also planted because of its unique appearance and interesting character when leafless against the blue winter sky. The Kenucky coffeetree's seeds, if roasted in time of poverty or penury, can be used as a pale substitute for coffee or chicory.

ALLEGHENY CHINQUAPIN—*CASTANEA PUMILA* (X#3-N°6): A small deciduous tree with a moderate growth rate that can be pruned to maintain a height of 15 feet. Captain John Smith, while adventuring upriver from Jamestown, encountered Pocahontas and the Allegheny chinquapin, observing the following: "The Indians have a small fruit growing on little trees, husked like a chestnut, but the fruit almost like a very small acorne. This they call Checkinquamins, which they esteem a great daintie." Today, Allegheny chinquapins are primarily used in landscapes for the purpose of attracting wildlife. While their nuts are smaller than regular chestnuts, they are reputed to be tastier and can be eaten fresh. The gray squirrels' love of these dwarf chestnuts keeps them scarce in the local produce markets.

BLACK GUM—*NYSSA SYLVATICA* (X#3-N°7): A medium-sized deciduous tree with a slow-to-moderate growth rate that can attain a 20-year height of 20 feet. The black gum tree, locally referred to as black tupelo, sour gum, cotton gum, swamp black gum, and yellow gum, isn't related to gum trees at all, gum trees being in the eucalyptus family. Because the wood of the black gum is very hard, it begins to decay at the top, the tree eventually hollows out, and its hollow trunks are often made into beehives rather than being used as firewood. The honey produced from the black gum's flowers, famously known as tupelo honey, is considered to be the Queen of the Honey World.

PRAIRIE CRAB APPLE—*MALUS IOENSIS* (X#3-N°8): A small deciduous tree, with a moderate minus growth rate, that can be pruned to maintain a height of 15 to 20 feet. The crab apple tree's namesake fruits are hard, bitter, edible, and can be transformed by the dexterous into a palatable jelly. The more discriminating prairie wildlife loves the whole tree, its fragrant flowers, its tasty foliage, and its succulent little crab apples. Come winter, the cottontail rabbit will browse on the bark of its saplings.

Shrubs

AMERICAN SMOKETREE—*COTINUS OBOVATUS* (X#3-N°9): A large deciduous shrub with a slow-to-moderate growth rate that can be trimmed to maintain a height of 10 feet. The American smoketree is a rare shrub that is possibly extinct in the wild. Its flowers, rather than its carbon emissions, are what give this shrub—or possibly small tree—its name. But the American smoketree's true horticultural fame lies with the bright color of its fall leaves, which are said to be fluorescent, as well as its gnarled limb structure and dark flaking bark. Its seeds are a choice food among the finches.

POSSUMHAW HOLLY—*ILEX DECIDUA* (X#3-N°10): A medium-sized deciduous shrub with a moderate growth rate that is best kept trimmed to a height of 6 to 8 feet. The possumhaw holly's berries stay red and on the branch all winter, while its leaves uncharacteristically fall off. The berries can be used as frugal, scrooge-like Christmas decorations or left dangling for the attending wildlife, inclusive of the opossum.

ROSESHELL AZALEA—*RHODODENDRON PRINOPHYLLUM* (X#3-N°11): A medium-sized deciduous shrub with a fast growth rate that is best kept trimmed to a height of 4 to 6 feet. The roseshell azalea's flowers are beautiful and smell like cloves. If its spent flowers are removed, in a horticultural surgical process called deadheading, more flowers will grow in their place.

VERNAL WITCH HAZEL—*HAMAMELIS VERNALIS* (X#3-N°12): A medium-sized deciduous shrub with a moderate growth rate that is best kept trimmed to a height of 4 to 6 feet. The vernal witch hazel flowers from late winter into early spring, when little else blooms and temperatures drop below freezing. The petals of its flowers curl up on very cold days, an adaptive mechanism that protects them from freeze damage. The vernal witch hazel's hard, woody fruit capsule, just ½ inch long, splits into a 2-parted tip in the early fall and, at some uncertain moment, the seeds are shot out to a distance of 30 feet.

WILD HYDRANGEA—*HYDRANGEA ARBORESCENS* (X#3-N°13): A medium- to minus-sized deciduous shrub with a moderate growth rate that is best kept trimmed to a height of 4 to 6 feet. Besides its famous flowers, the wild hydrangea's stem bark has a peculiar tendency to peel off in several successive layers, hence its common name seven bark. Both the indigenous and invasive peoples used concoctions of the wild hydrangea's roots as a remedy for minor ailments and maladies.

BLACKBERRY—*RUBUS SP.* (X#3-N°14): A medium-sized deciduous shrub with a moderate to fast growth rate that is best kept trimmed to a height of 4 to 6 feet. The blackberry's berries are delicious, but they are only produced on 1-year-old canes (stems). Therefore, after a cane bears fruit, it must be cut down so that others may rise in its place and bear more berries. What distinguishes the blackberry from its raspberry relatives is that the torus, the berry's internal stem, picks with the berry. As the torus can be bitter, some nibble around it when eating the berry raw. For finicky eaters, the problem is easily resolved by cooking. Blackberries do not ripen after they are picked, and they are red when unripe, hence the expression "blackberries are red when they are green."

AMERICAN SNOWBELL—*STYRIX AMERICANGUS* (X#3-N°15): A medium-sized deciduous shrub with a moderate growth rate that is best kept trimmed to a height of 4 to 6 feet. The American snowbell is a shrub of subtle, elegant beauty as its leaves are dark green, its bark is gray to reddish brown, and its pendulous white bell-shaped flowers—snowbells—droop from the branches in early spring. Its spring flowers give way to small fruits in fall.

Ground Cover and Wildflowers

WILD PETUNIA—*RUELLIA HUMILUS* (X#3-N°16): A perennial flowering herb that thrives in shade and can attain heights of 6 to 12 inches. While the wild petunia resembles the cultivated petunia, they are members of different plant families. Their lavender flowers, which bloom from July to late September, have no noticeable scent and open during the morning and fall off by evening. These flowers have unusually fine purple lines that radiate from the center to function as nectar guides for visiting pollinators.

SAND PHLOX—*PHLOX BIFIDA* (X#3-N°17): A low-spreading, ground-hugging, evergreen herb with pale purple starlike flowers that can attain heights of between 4 and 6 inches. Sand phlox is both a useful and beautiful ground cover because it spreads evenly and quickly. Moreover, an impressive variety of Missouri butterflies, moths, and skippers drink the flower's nectar, while an equally large array of other wildlife feast on its foliage.

FALSE RUE ANEMONE—*ISOPYRUM BITERNATUM* (X#3-N°18): A delicate-looking perennial herb that can attain heights of between 5 and 8 inches. The false rue anemone's main claim to ground cover fame is that it is regularly confused with another similar-looking plant. Still, the false rue anemone is a tough woodland creature that flowers in spring and whose leaves last well into the season. It merits a place in the shade, if not in the sun.

BUFFALO GRASS—*BOUTELOUA DACTYLOIDES* (X#3-N°19): A perennial grass that can attain a height of 5 to 7 inches. Buffalo grass, the only native grass that could be categorized as a turf grass, is named for the buffalo that used to graze on it. With the quasi-extinction of the buffalo, several species of grasshoppers have kept up the old traditions. If used in the front yard, buffalo grass could require periodic mowing.

LITTLE BLUESTEM—*SCHIZACHYRIUM SCOPARIUM* (X#3-N°20): A small, non-spreading, clump-forming grass that attains a height of 24 to 36 inches. Typical of the mixed and tall grass prairies, the little bluestem is a warm season clump grass with a dense root system. Its thin leaves turn bright red in fall and have a fluffy silver-white seed stalk. In recent antiquity, its cousin, the big bluestem, was largely responsible for the formation of the famous prairie sod. Like all native prairie grasses, little bluestem provides food, cover, and habitat for wildlife.

MISSOURI BLACK-EYED SUSAN—*RUDBECKIA MISSOURIENSIS* (X#3-N°21): A perennial daisy-like wildflower that can attain a height between 18 and 24 inches. Blooming mainly in summer, with their signature yellow to orange petals and a dark center point, the Missouri black-eyed Susan has a strong root system that often allows the plant to rejuvenate itself each year. Its bright orange-yellow petals have a unique way of reflecting the sun's ultraviolet rays, waves invisible to the human eye, which attract those bees that can see and appreciate this spectrum.

PURPLE CONEFLOWER—*ECHINACEA PURPUREA* (X#3-N°22): A perennial purple wildflower with cone-like heads on top of wiry stems that can attain heights of between 12 and 24 inches. A veteran tall grass prairie forb, the purple coneflower is scientifically named after the purple sea urchin (*Echinacea*) that learned botanists thought its flowers resembled. The real or imagined healing powers of the purple coneflower's dried and powdered roots seem to have worked their way into the entire apothecary of tribal and folk medicines. The Missouri goldfinch, heedless of the needs of an afflicted human population, eats the purple coneflower's cone-shaped seeds as fast as they ripen.

PURPLE MILKWEED—*ASCLEPIAS PURPURAS-CENS* (X#3-N°23): A perennial, non-spreading, purple wildflower that can attain heights of between 30 and 48 inches. Another milkweed that is essential for the survival of the monarch butterfly as well as supplying nectar for a host of other pollinators, the purple milkweed is particularly adapted to life on the prairie as it grows higher than competing species of milkweeds and has more striking flowers.

PURPLE PRAIRIE CLOVER—*PALEA PURPUREA* (X#3-N°24): A perennial, grasslike wildflower that can attain heights of between 2 and 3 feet. Once an important component of the entire midwestern prairie system, the purple prairie clover is a nitrogen-fixing plant with abundant, purple, cone-like flowers. During purple prairie clover's early growth stages, its foliage has high nutritional value for a wide range of wildlife. After flowering, its seeds are avidly consumed by birds and small mammals.

MISSOURI PRIMROSE—*OENOTHERA MACRO-CARPA* (X#3-N°25): A trailing perennial wildflower that can attain heights of between 6 and 10 inches. The Missouri primrose's large yellow flowers, sometimes 4 inches in diameter, bloom from spring through summer, with each flower lasting but a single day.

PASTURE ROSE—*ROSA CAROLINA* (X#3-N°26): A perennial wildflower that can attain heights of between 12 and 24 inches. The pasture rose's large fragrant pink flowers bloom in June and July and give way to bright red rose hips in the late summer.

These rose hips then become an important food source for wildlife in winter. The petals are edible and said to be good on salads.

SPIDER MILKWEED—*ASCLEPIAS VIRIDIS* (X#3-N°27): A perennial, early-blooming wildflower with large yellow and green flowers that attain heights of between 18 and 24 inches. One cannot have too many milkweeds, and the monarch butterfly desires them all. The spider milkweed has a special attraction for hummingbirds, blooming early in spring, before other flowers are available.

EXERCISE #4: PLANTS NATIVE TO THE SOUTHWEST

Trees

BALD CYPRESS—*TAXODIUM DISTICHUM AMERICANA* (X#4-N°1): A medium- to plus-sized deciduous tree with a fast growth rate when young but that slows down as the tree matures. The bald cypress forests that once dominated the East Texas swamps contained specimens that were well over a thousand years old. Bald cypress trees that evolved in a swamp exhibit two particularities that are less common to those growing on dry land. The first particularity is a growth called cypress knees, which are woody projections from the root system that rise above the water or land. The second particularity is that the tree trunk is thicker at its base, called a buttressed trunk. The most likely explanation for these features is that they provide the tree with extra stability during high winds and floods. Even hurricanes rarely overturn bald cypress trees.

YAUPON HOLLY—*ILEX VOMITORIA* (X#4-N°2): A small evergreen tree with a moderate growth rate that can attain a 20-year height of

18 feet. The southeastern native tribes made a brew of the yaupon holly's leaves and stems for use in a boy's initiation into manhood, a ceremony that included the initiate's vomiting. The yaupon holly's scientific epithet—*vomitoria*—comes from a European's incorrect assumption that it was its chemical composition that caused the vomiting, rather than the excessive amounts of the foul brew the initiates were required to imbibe as proof of their budding manhood. In truth, almost any foul brew consumed in mad excess after fasting and submission to dark and troubling rites is a sure path toward vomiting. The leaves of the yaupon holly have the highest caffeine content of any plant native to America and, if lightly brewed and consumed in moderation, the resulting libation is a miserable substitute for coffee.

BLACK WILLOW—*SALEX NIGRA* (X#4-N°3):
A medium-sized deciduous tree with a moderate growth rate, that can attain a 20-year height of 20 feet. The black willow, or swamp willow as the *S. nigra* is locally called, is another denizen of the swamp that has found new use as an environmental restorative. The black willow is not only able to survive persistent flooding, but has a tenacious spreading root system that becomes a formidable erosion-control tool. It is also one of the first plants to flower and to provide bees, hungry after a long flowerless winter, with nectar and pollen.

WATER TUPELO—*NYSSA AQUATICA* (X#4-N°4):
A medium- to plus-sized deciduous tree with a moderate growth rate that can attain a 20-year height of 20 feet. Commonly found in swampland, *Nyssa*, water tupelo's genus name, refers to Greek freshwater nymphs of uneven morals and dangerous reputations. Like many swamp dwellers, water tupelo is perfectly at home in suburbia and produces large barely edible fruits that are best left for the wildlife.

DRUMMOND'S RED MAPLE—*ACER RUBRUM DRUMMONDII* (X#4-N°5): A
medium- to plus-sized deciduous tree with a fast growth rate that can attain a 20-year height of 30 feet. When botanists, traditionally a sedate group, gather, and the genus *Acer rubrum* is invoked, Drummond's red maple becomes a topic of heated debate. The liberal botanists consider the Drummond a runaway species of maple, bred in the swamp, and of uncertain parentage, whereas the more conservative botanists claim that it is merely an adaptive variety. Whether adopted or adapted, the Drummond red maple has the same colorful fall foliage as its relatives.

SOUTHERN LIVE OAK—*QUERCUS VIRGINIANA* (X#4-N°6): A large evergreen tree with
a moderate growth rate that can attain a 20-year height of 25 feet. Not a true evergreen, the southern live oak retains its leaves nearly year-round and sheds them just before the new leaves appear in spring. Its wood is hard, heavy, and difficult to work with, but very strong. In the time of wooden ships, live oaks were the preferred source of framework timbers. The USS *Constitution*, built from southern live oak, was able to sustain heavy cannon fire, earning her the name Old Ironsides. Today, southern live oaks are protected and planted to provide food and shelter for the wildlife and shade for the overheated.

PEPPERWOOD—*ZANTHOXYLUM CLAVA-HERCULIS* (X#4-N°7): A small to minus-sized
deciduous tree with a moderate growth rate that can attain a 20-year height of 15 feet. The pepperwood tree, due to its peculiar, spiked bark, is often referred to as Hercules Club. It is also called the toothache tree or tingle tongue because chewing on its leaves, bark, or twigs causes a tingling numbness of the mouth, tongue, teeth, and gums. In the past, this numb-

ing characteristic made it a popular remedy for a toothache, and one can still purchase various concoctions made from it. Roasted, the pepperwood's red berries are one of the main ingredients in Sichuan seasoning.

MEXICAN PLUM—*PRUNUS MEXICANA* (X#4-N°8): A medium- to minus-sized deciduous tree with a moderate growth rate that can attain a 20-year height of 15 feet. The Mexican plum tree's inclusion in many gardens is due to the beauty and fragrance of its flowers, rather than the tastiness of its plums. The plums are best left for the wildlife, or even the compost pit in a productive season. Yet, it is rumored that in some seasons, these plums can be teased into a decent jelly.

Shrubs

CORAL BERRY—*SYMPHORICARPOS ORBICULATUS* (X#4-N°9): A small to plus-sized deciduous shrub with a moderate growth rate that is best kept trimmed to a height of 4 feet. As the coral berry's fruits contain a chemical highly toxic to fish, the crafty American Indians would crush its berries, throw them into a stream or lake, and harvest the stunned fish that floated up to the surface. The coral berry's complicated root systems make it an excellent plant for erosion control on slopes.

TEXAS LANTANA—*LANTANA URTICOIDES* (X#4-N°10): A small deciduous shrub with a moderate growth rate that is best kept trimmed to a height of between 4 to 6 feet. Texas lantana is a hardy local shrub that massively flowers all summer long and through part of fall. Butterflies, birds, and bees love its nectar and fruits, and it is not troubled by 100-degree weather. When young, Texas lantana should be pruned down to 12 to 18 inches before the start of winter so that it develops a strong lower branch system.

WAX MYRTLE—*MYRICA CERIFERA* (X#4-N°11): A large to plus-sized evergreen shrub with a moderate growth rate that is best kept trimmed to a height of 6 feet. The wax myrtle is a swamp dweller with erosion-resistant roots and a fragrant background. The early colonists boiled the berries to recover their waxy outer coverings to make scented candles. A bird's digestive system can also remove the wax from the fruit, a prerequisite for germination.

CHILE PEQUIN—*CAPSICUM FRUTSCENS* (X#4-N°12): A small to plus-sized deciduous shrub with a moderate growth rate that is best kept trimmed to a height of between 4 and 6 feet. The chile pequin's peppers are ripe when they are red and on the hot side, but the birds do not seem to mind the heat. A highly valued seasoning, chile pequin peppers cost more than 10 times the price of many other peppers.

ROUGHLEAF DOGWOOD—*CORNUA DRUMMONDII* (X#4-N°13): A large deciduous shrub with a moderate growth rate that is best kept trimmed to a height of between 6 and 8 feet. While the roughleaf dogwood is not overly ornamental, at least 40 species of birds are known to feast on its fruits, and almost every native bee feeds on its nectar and pollen. Come nighttime, the nocturnal wildlife gets in line for their chance at the shrub's goodies.

VIRGINIA SWEETSPIRE—*ITEA VIRGINICA* (X#4-N°14): A medium-sized deciduous shrub with a moderate growth rate that is best kept trimmed to a height of between 4 and 6 feet. The Virginia sweetspire, in the southern part of its range, is semi-evergreen. In the wild, it grows best in swamps and wooded stream banks, where its root systems provide a remedy for erosion.

SOUTHERN DEWBERRY—*RUBRUS TRIVIALIS* (X#4-N°15): A small evergreen shrub with a moderate growth rate that is best kept trimmed to a height of between 3 and 4 feet. The southern dewberry is essentially a low-growing, purplish, blackberry bush, except that it only produces a single flower per little branch, thus a single berry. Fortunately, there are a lot of little branches to pick from and they are less thorny than their darker cousins. When ripe, dewberries are slightly sweeter than blackberries and are delicious eaten raw, baked into pies, or made into jam.

Ground Cover

PIGEONBERRY—*RIVINIA HUMILIS* (X#4-N°16): A spreading perennial evergreen herb that thrives in the shade and can attain a height of 18 inches. The pigeonberry produces flowers and berries at the same time, from spring through fall, both of which are sought-after wildlife treats. Shade-loving, the pigeonberry thrives particularly well under the southern live oak.

TEXAS FROGFRUIT—*PHYLA NODIFLORA* (X#4-N°17): A spreading semi-evergreen herb that thrives in boggy areas and can attain a height of 18 inches. The Texas frogfruit's small white-to-pink flowers take on a match-like appearance, which explains why the plant is sometimes called matchweed. It will grow in almost any soil and can tolerate foot traffic, but it will not tolerate mowing.

POWDERPUFF MIMOSA—*MIMOSA STRIG-ILLOSA* (X#4-N°18): A fast-spreading semi-evergreen perennial that can attain heights of between 6 and 8 inches. The powderpuff mimosa gets its name from the small, spherical flowers that rise above the plant's creeping vines. Because of the powderpuff's mat-forming nature, its capacity to fix nitrogen in the soil, and its ability to withstand foot traffic and even mowing, it behaves in many of the same ways as turf grass.

Wildflowers

ANTELOPE HORNS—*ACCLEPIAS ASPERULE* (X#4-N°19): A spreading perennial wildflower that can attain heights of between 8 and 24 inches. Of the 100 or more species of milkweed in America, over 30 of them are native to Texas, and antelope horns are one of the most important for the monarchs flying over the Lone Star State. They get their name from their seedpods, which look similar to the horns of an antelope.

GREEN MILKWEED—*ACCLEPIAS VIRIDIS* (X#4-N°20): A spreading perennial wildflower that can attain heights of between 24 and 36 inches. Green milkweed is the most common milkweed in East Texas. It typically has wider leaves than other milkweeds and white flowers, often just one per plant.

TEXAS MILKWEED—*ACCLEPIAS TEXANA* (X#4-N°21): A spreading perennial wildflower that can attain heights of between 12 and 18 inches. Texas milkweed is one of the more attractive milkweeds to the gardener; it has slender leaves and tiny snowball-like flowers that bloom from May to August.

TEXAS INDIAN PAINTBRUSH—*CASTILLEJA INDIVISA* (X#4-N°22): Sometimes an annual or biennial wildflower that can attain heights of between 8 and 18 inches. The roots of the Texas Indian paintbrush will grow until they touch the roots of other plants, after which their roots penetrate the host roots to obtain a portion of the host plant's nutrients. It has bright red paintbrush-like bracts that attract hummingbirds.

TEXAS BLUEBONNET—*LUPINUS TEXENSIS* (X#4-N°23): An annual wildflower that grows to heights between 12 and 18 inches. Texas bluebonnets begin their lives as small, gravel-like seeds that must be penetrated by wind or rain over the course of a few months in order to germinate. As such, East Texas is a happy home for this particular bluebonnet, although all five species of bluebonnets are recognized as the Texas state flower.

LADY BIRD JOHNSON LEGACY WILDFLOWER MIX: The wife of the 36th president of the United States and the nation's premier wildflower advocate, Lady Bird Johnson correctly observed that "where flowers bloom, so does hope." In 1994, she founded the Lady Bird Johnson Wildflower Center, an organization dedicated to preserving and reintroducing native plants in planned landscapes. The LBJ Center sells Lady Bird's Legacy Wildflower Mix, a mix that has become a must for all reputable Texas wildflower gardens.

EXERCISE #5: PLANTS NATIVE TO THE WEST

Trees

VALLEY OAK—*QUERCUS LOBATA* (X#5-N°1): A large deciduous tree with a very fast growth rate that can attain a 20-year height of 60 feet. Endemic to the Central Valley, the aptly named valley oak is the largest of all American oak trees. While the valley oak can tolerate many climactic variables, it must have year-round access to groundwater. Unlike other oaks, their most characteristic community is not one of dense, mixed-species woodland, but rather an open savannah where each tree can spread out horizontally without competing for sunlight from others. Its extremely large acorns are edible, albeit difficult to hull and mash, and were a staple food of the indigenous tribes.

BLACK ELM—*ULMUS AMERICANA* (X#5-N°2): A large deciduous tree, not native to California, with a fast growth rate that can attain a 20-year height of 25 feet. Native to the eastern United States, black elm trees—beautiful, fast-growing, and sturdy—were planted almost everywhere west of the Mississippi from the mid-1800s on. Their popularity led to overplanting, and overplanting produced a monoculture of elms that had no resistance to disease. In the 1930s, Dutch elm disease (DED) struck and there was no cure. By 1989, 75% of the estimated 77 million elm trees in the United States had been lost. DED was first detected in Sacramento in 1990, but the city has made great efforts to keep its black elm tree population healthy.

VINE MAPLE—*ACER CIRCINATUM* (X#5-N°3): A small deciduous tree with a fast growth rate that can attain a 20-year height of 20 feet. The vine maple is the perfect understory tree; it thrives in shade and has the same brilliant fall colors as its taller cousins. Not that everyone appreciates this plant in the wild, particularly hunters; its branches spread low next to the ground and can form a dense thicket. Its common name, vine, comes from the trees attractively gnarled and crooked trunk system.

WESTERN REDBUD—*CERCIS OCCIDENTALIS* (X#5-N°4): A small deciduous tree with a moderate growth rate that can attain a 20-year height of 15 feet. The western redbud is more densely twiggy and drought resistant than its eastern cousin, albeit equally beautiful to the beholder and useful for the habitat.

CALIFORNIA BUCKEYE—*AESCULUS CALIFORNICA* (X#5-N°5): A small deciduous tree with a moderate growth rate that can attain a 20-year height of 15 feet. The California buckeye has no charms to offer the invasive honeybee, which will avoid its flowers. Not so for the native bees, butterflies, hummingbirds, and sundry other pollinators, which are particularly attracted. The California buckeye likes the shade, squirrels like its nuts, and its gnarly white trunks and low branches make an attractive privacy screen in every season.

Shrubs

DEERBUSH—*CEANOTHUS INTEGERRIMUS* (X#5-N°6): A flowering deciduous, but sometimes evergreen, shrub with a fast growth rate that is best kept trimmed to heights of 4 to 6 feet. The deerbush is a lilac (*Ceanothus*) with an upright form, woody stems, and fragrant white, lavender, and blue flowers that bloom in winter and spring. The flowers are particularly attractive to bees and butterflies.

BUCK BRUSH—*CEANOTHUS CUNEATUS* (X#5-N°7): A flowering evergreen shrub with a fast growth rate that is best kept trimmed to a height of between 4 and 6 feet. The buck brush, particularly attractive to bees and butterflies, is a lilac with an upright form, woody stems, and fragrant white flowers, sometimes tinted with lavender and blue.

HAIRY CEANOTHUS—*CEANOTHUS OLI-GANTHUS* (X#5-N°8): A flowering evergreen shrub with a fast growth rate that is best kept trimmed to a height of between 4 to 6 feet. The hairy ceanothus lilac has a mounding form, woody stems, and clusters of blue and white flowers that bloom in winter and spring. The fruits (seeds) are attractive to birds.

LEMMON'S CEANOTHUS—*CEANOTHUS OLI-GANTHUS* (X#5-N°9): A low-growing evergreen shrub with a fast growth rate that is best kept trimmed to a height of between 3 and 4 feet. If left untrimmed, Lemmon's ceanothus can appear to be a ground cover, with its spreading form, dull green leaves, and purplish-blue flowers.

CALIFORNIA ALLSPICE—*CALYCANTHUS OCCIDENTALIS* (X#5-N°10): A flowering deciduous shrub with a fast growth rate that is best kept trimmed to a height of between 4 and 6 feet. The California allspice is often called sweetshrub, because its leaves can be as fragrant as its flowers. The scent has been compared to apples cooked with cinnamon.

CALIFORNIA ANEMONE—*CARPENTERIA CALIFORNICA* (X#5-N°11): A flowering evergreen shrub with a fast growth rate that is best kept trimmed to a height of between 4 and 6 feet. The California anemone's anemone-shaped, scented flowers are glistening white and, as a member of the mock-orange family, it is worth growing just for its attractive foliage.

OREGON GRAPE—*MAHONIA AQUIFOLIUM* (X#5-N°12): A flowering evergreen shrub with a fast growth rate that is best kept trimmed to a height of between 4 and 6 feet. The Oregon grape's yellow flowers give way to dark bluish-black berries that are quite tart and contain large seeds. While these fruits can be used to make jelly, or even eaten raw after the first frost, they are best left for the birds.

CALIFORNIA ROSE—*ROSA CALIFORNICA* (X#5-N°13): A flowering deciduous shrub with a fast growth rate that is best kept trimmed to a height of between 4 to 6 feet. The California rose is a thicket-forming shrub whose purple flowers give way to bright red rose hips that are often dried for tea or used in jams or jellies. Because the rose hips remain on the plant throughout winter, they provide food for wildlife when little forage is available.

Vines and Ground Cover

BEARBERRY—*ARCTOSTAPHYLOS UVA-URSI* (X#5-N°14): A prostrate evergreen ground cover with a moderate growth rate that attains heights of between 2 and 5 inches. The bearberry's green summer foliage turns red or purplish in winter before turning green again in spring. Its fruits provide food for birds all winter, and its flowers attract hummingbirds in spring.

CARPET MANZANITA—*ARCTOSTAPHYLOS EMERALD CARPET* (X#5-N°15): A prostrate evergreen ground cover with a moderate growth rate that attains heights of between 4 and 8 inches. A natural hybrid, not a cultivar, the carpet manzanita has the color and richness of a lawn without being too tread-worthy. The Spanish settlers named these plants because their berries resembled apples; manzanita translates as "little apples."

CALIFORNIA WILD GRAPE—*VITUS CALIFORNICA* (X#5-N°16): A fast-growing deciduous vine that can attain lengths of over 30 feet. A member of Gabriel Moraga's 1808 expedition to the Central Valley wrote of their discovery of the Sacramento River: "Canopies of oaks and cottonwoods, many festooned with grape vines, overhung both sides of the blue current. Birds chattered in the trees and big fish darted through the pellucid depths." The festoons the Spaniards were looking at were certainly those of the California wild grape, which continues to flourish on the banks of the same river. Its grapes are small, often sour, but edible, and can be teased into a mediocre jelly. Given that these grapes are an important food source for a variety of wildlife, birds in particular, it is better if they are left on the vine.

Wildflowers

CALIFORNIA POPPY—*ESCHSCHOLIZIA CALIFORNICA* (X#5-N°17): An annual wildflower that can attain a height of between 12 and 18 inches. The California poppy, California's official state flower, will sprout the following year from its own roots and stems. Look for native bees scrambling around the bottom of the bloom while covering themselves with pollen.

TUFTED POPPY—*ESCHSCHOLIZIA CAESPITASA* (X#5-N°18): A wildflower that will reseed itself while attaining heights of 12 to 18 inches. The tufted poppy is soft to the touch, with tidy foliage and scented primrose flowers. The flowers open and close with the sun, but on windy or cloudy days, the petals may remain closed.

NARROWLEAF MILKWEED—*ASCLEPIAS FASCICULARIS* (X#5-N°19): A perennial wildflower with narrow leaves that often whorl about its stem. Narrowleaf milkweed blooms with clusters of lavender-tinted white flowers and is the single most important host plant for monarch butterflies in the Central Valley.

EXERCISE #6: PLANTS NATIVE TO THE NORTHWEST

Trees

WESTERN RED CEDAR—*THUJA PLICATA* (X#6-N°1): A large evergreen tree with a fast growth rate that can attain a 20-year height of 25 feet. As the buffalo was to the Plains Indian, gold to the Spanish invader, and the musket to the early settlers, so the western red cedar was to the Northwest American Indian. The coastal tribes made use of this venerable tree[*] from cradle to grave and beyond. The red cedar's close-grained, aromatic, rot-resistant wood was used for building cradles, dishes, boxes, houses, canoes, totem poles, and coffins. The tree's bark

---

[*] The red cedar can live for 1,000 years.

was used to make clothing, baskets, mats, and salmon traps. The tree's aromatic foliage was used as a drug for various ailments, and men chewed on its branch tips to avoid nausea when burying the dead.

RED ALDER—*ALNUS RUBRA* (X#6-N°2): A medium-sized deciduous tree with a fast growth rate that can attain a 20-year height of 30 feet. The first botanical observation of the red alder appears in the journals of Lewis and Clark, the former being quite keen on the subject of botany and who described a fair specimen of a red alder growing near their winter camp. Other than being vital to yesterday's coastal tribes and today's habitat, the red alder has the unique ability to create its own fertilizer.

PACIFIC MADRONE—*ARBUTUS MENZIE-SII* (X#6-N°3): A medium-sized evergreen tree with a fast growth rate that can attain a 20-year height of 25 feet. When mature, the Pacific madrone's bark peels away in thin sheets, leaving the new bark lustrous and smooth. In spring, it bears flowers that will give way to red berries in fall. When the berries dry out, they have a hooked barb that will catch onto larger animals for migration. The Pacific madrone also provides an important nesting site for many birds.

BIGLEAF MAPLE—*ACER MACROPHYLLUM SERICEA* (X#6-N°4): A medium- to plus-sized deciduous tree with a fast growth rate, particularly when juvenile, that can attain a 20-year height of 25 feet. Called bigleaf because it has the largest leaves of all maples, some of which attain lengths of over 20 inches. The bark of the bigleaf maple supports the growth of certain mosses and lichens, all of which are beneficial to the ecosystem and none of which compromise the trees' health. On a culinary note, its flowers are edible, quite sweet, and great in salads.

RED TWIG DOGWOOD—*CORNUS SERICEA* (X#6-N°5): A small deciduous tree with a moderate growth rate that can attain a 20-year height of 15 feet. The red twig dogwood, unlike its eastern cousins, is often planted for its showy red twigs in the winter season, rather than for its colorful bracts in spring.

Shrubs

PACIFIC RHODODENDRON—*RHODODENDRON MACROPHYLLUM* (X#6-N°6): An evergreen shrub with a fast growth rate that is best kept trimmed to a height of between 4 and 10 feet. The Pacific rhododendron is Washington's state flower and state shrub. Its large whorls of flowers are usually pink, and its leaves are always deep green, as it sheds them every few years. The Pacific rhododendron may have the dubious distinction of being the only plant that the crafty coastal tribes found no use for.

COMMON JUNIPER—*JUNIPERUS COMMUNISUS* (X#6-N°7): An evergreen conifer with a fast growth rate that is very variable in form. The common juniper can range from a medium- to minus-sized tree, 30 to 40 feet tall, to a low, often prostrate spreading shrub just a foot or two off the ground. Its astringent blue-black seed cones, known as juniper berries once they have dried, can be used to flavor meats, sauces, beers, and, famously, gin, *gin* being a word derived from the old French term for juniper. As the juniper's seed cones need more than a year to ripen, the same tree/shrub will have both ripe and unripe cones at the same time.

SITKA MOUNTAIN ASH—*SORBUS SITCHENSIS* (X#6-N°8): A medium-sized deciduous shrub with a fast growth rate that is best kept trimmed to a height of between 4 and 6 feet. The

Sitka mountain ash is an aromatic shrub that produces clusters of small white flowers and round red berries that remain on the branch throughout winter, all to better nourish the wildlife that, in turn, distribute its seeds.

BITTER CHERRY—*PRUNUS EMARGINATA* (X#6-N°9): A medium-sized flowering deciduous shrub with a fast growth rate that is best trimmed to a height of between 4 and 6 feet. The bitter cherry's fruit is a juicy red or purple cherry color and, as its name forebodes, is indeed bitter. What the bitter cherry's name does not suggest, nor does the appearance of its delicious-looking berries, is that it is inedible for humans but not so for wildlife.

SALAL—*GAULTHERIA SHALLON* (X#6-N°10): A medium-sized flowering evergreen shrub with a fast growth rate that is best kept trimmed to a height of between 4 and 6 feet. Salal is a member of the heather family, and its dark blue berries and young leaves are both edible and efficient appetite suppressants, making them doubly useful for the summer tourists that get hopelessly lost while exploring the forests of Puget Sound.

BALDHIP ROSE—*ROSA GYMNOCARPA* (X#6-N°11): A medium-sized flowering deciduous shrub with a fast growth rate that is best kept trimmed to a height of between 4 and 6 feet. The baldhip rose, whose petals fall off the hip earlier than its peers, is a very attractive shrub to pollinators and also provides food and shelter to a large variety of birds and animals.

Vines and Ground Cover

TRUMPET HONEYSUCKLE—*LONICERA CILIOSA* (X#6-N°12): A flowering deciduous vine with a fast growth rate that can climb to a height of over 10 feet. The trumpet honeysuck-

le's common name, honeysuckle, comes from the fact that children enjoy sucking the nectar from the base of the flower. Its bright red flowers are also a favorite of hummingbirds.

PINK HONEYSUCKLE—*LONICERA HISPIDULA* (X#6-N°13): A flowering deciduous vine/shrub with a fast growth rate that can climb to a height of over 8 feet. The pink honeysuckle grows as a loose and low shrub until its branches come into contact with something it can twine onto, like a neighboring plant or a fence, from where its branches will twine upward.

CREEPING DOGWOOD—*CORNUS CANADENSIS* (X#6-N°14): An herbaceous perennial ground cover with a slow growth rate that stays within heights of between 4 and 8 inches. Unlike its relatives, trees for the most part and shrubs for the lesser part, the creeping dogwood sticks to the forest floor, generally forming a carpet-like mat. During late spring and the early summer months, the creeping dogwood has highly elastic white petals that flip backward, releasing springy filaments that are cocked underneath. The filaments then snap upward, flinging pollen out of containers hinged to the filaments. The stamen accelerates at a rate of about 80,000 feet a second and the pollen experiences 2,000 to 3,000 times the force of gravity. Curiously, the usual pollinators are not distracted by this rapid behavior.

TWIN FLOWER—*LINNAEA BOREALIS* (X#6-N°15): A prostrate perennial flowering ground cover with a moderate growth rate that stays within heights of 6 to 12 inches. The twin flower is a waif of a plant, found throughout the northern hemisphere in the colder circumboreal habitats. Despite its Ice Age–old penchant for cold, dark forests, the twin flower seems to have no particular habitat preference and will thrive happily in a suburban yard. The twin flower was a favorite of another famous circumboreal habitant, Carl Linnaeus, for whom the flower was named.

SHOWY MILKWEED—*ASCLEPIAS SPECIOSA* (X#6-N°16): An erect perennial wildflower with hirsute pale pink to purplish pink flowers that can attain a height of between 2 and 3 feet.

The tonsorially challenged showy milkweed is the preferred milkweed of the western monarch butterfly. The western monarch, like its cousins in the Midwestern and Eastern states, is in deep trouble due to a declining availability of milkweed. It is worth mentioning that because there are no native milkweeds just to the east of the Cascade Mountains, there can be no monarch butterflies.

NEXT PAGE, FROM TOP: Sweetshrub; Downy serviceberry

INDEX

"Honeybee"

"Spotted

Goldfinch

"Northern Cardinal"